THE WAR DIARIES
of a
TEENAGE GAL

1939 *to* 1945

¤

For my parents
who always took most loving care of me

MONIACK BOOKS

THE WAR DIARIES *of a* TEENAGE GAL

1939 *to* **1945**

¤

PHILIPPA GUISE *now* **FRASER**

Quo honestior eo tutior

The more honest is the more safe

Motto of the Guises of Elmore

THE WAR DIARIES *of a* TEENAGE GAL 1939 to 1945

First published in the United Kingdom in 2013 by Moniack Books, Moniack Castle, Kirkhill IV5 7PQ.

Typeset in Constantia and printed and bound in England by Berforts Information Press, Hertfordshire.

ISBN 978-1-908616-47-0

Acknowledgements

My thanks go to my daughter Sophia Yates who made the first typescript from my manuscript diaries, and to her husband Robin who has spent days checking all I wrote in these diaries, has put in many of the footnotes (the credit for which, he insists, may be shared with many nameless internet contributors), and laid it all out in the present format and designed the cover. Robin's footnotes are absolutely terrific and add immensely to the interest of this book.

Contents

List of Illustrations

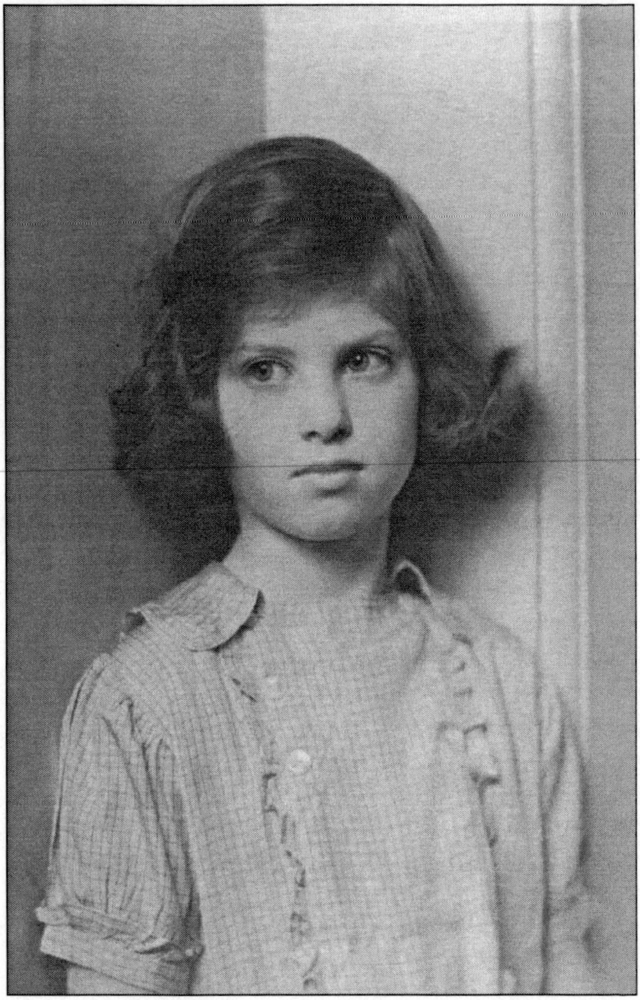

Philippa Guise – the Gal – in 1935, aged nine.

1

Introduction: Waving at the Zeppelin

I shall begin by painting a picture of my life before the war.

We had a German governess, Fräulein Weiss, whom I and my family loved greatly. I lived with my father, mother and two younger brothers, and with Fräulein Weiss and a house full of servants, at Elmore Court, the Guise family's ancient seat in the idyllic Gloucestershire village of Elmore.[1] Fräulein Weiss had come to us in 1935, when I was nine.

One of my sharpest memories from soon before the war is of the first week of August 1939, two months after I had become a teenager, when I was out on the lawn at Elmore with my family and Fräulein. As we were playing, from nowhere a German Zeppelin flew low over the house. My brothers John and Jamie, and I, waved madly at it while my father, Sir Anselm, became furious, even saying he was sure that Fräulein must be a Nazi spy! To us three children it was a magical surprise. We could not have known that in these last few

[1] The Guise motto *Quo honestior eo tutior* has supplied the superscription to this edition of Philippa's diary.

weeks of peace we had been waving at and cheering-on the Graf Zeppelin II airship as she sailed back to Germany from a spying mission on Britain's early-warning radar defences, and that Elmore Court may even have been one of the navigator's landmarks guiding the airship home. [2]

Elmore Court, Gloucestershire.

Fräulein Weiss and Graf Zeppelin II were not the only German characters at Elmore in those years. My mother had a German Jewish parlour maid, Louisa, who had come to England as a refugee. She had a father in Germany and a sister in

---

[2] The only German airship to fly over Britain after World War One was the Graf Zeppelin II on her spying mission of August 2nd to 3rd, 1939. The outbound flight took the Zeppelin up Britain's east coast to Aberdeen after which she drifted westward and south until crossing the English Channel.

Amsterdam and another sister in Brussels. Fräulein was sure Louisa was lying about the Nazis, believing Hitler to be marvellous and singing the praises of the Hitler Youth, the Führer's autobahns and all that Adolf had achieved for Germany. Fräulein wished us children to admire him just as she admired him, and once took us to see a newsreel of Hitler giving a very noisy speech and making the "Heil Hitler" salute with his outstretched arm.

Another time Fräulein took us to Harrods to show us the miracle of television, so soon before all the screens were to go dark, the broadcasts ending so that TV signals might not guide German bombers towards London. It was April 1939 when I stood with Fräulein watching that miracle of television – it was a broadcast about the Spanish Civil War in which German airpower had been such a decisive and destructive factor.

Elmore was very old fashioned, even in the 1930s, and very rural. The village of Elmore was (as it is to this day) part of the Guise family estate. The village had seven farms and a number of tied cottages, and was home to about 300 souls. When we drove through the village with my grandmother, Granny Guise (the Lady Guise of the day), who was much loved, the men would lift their caps and their wives give a little curtsy. To the villagers I was "Miss

Philippa", and my brothers "Master John" and "Master Jamie".

We knew everyone in the village, and my mother, Margaret, and grandmother often visited the school. My mother belonged to the Mother's Union church organisation. Every Sunday we walked across the fields to our village church, listening to the church bells ringing. The adults often went by car, and there was a

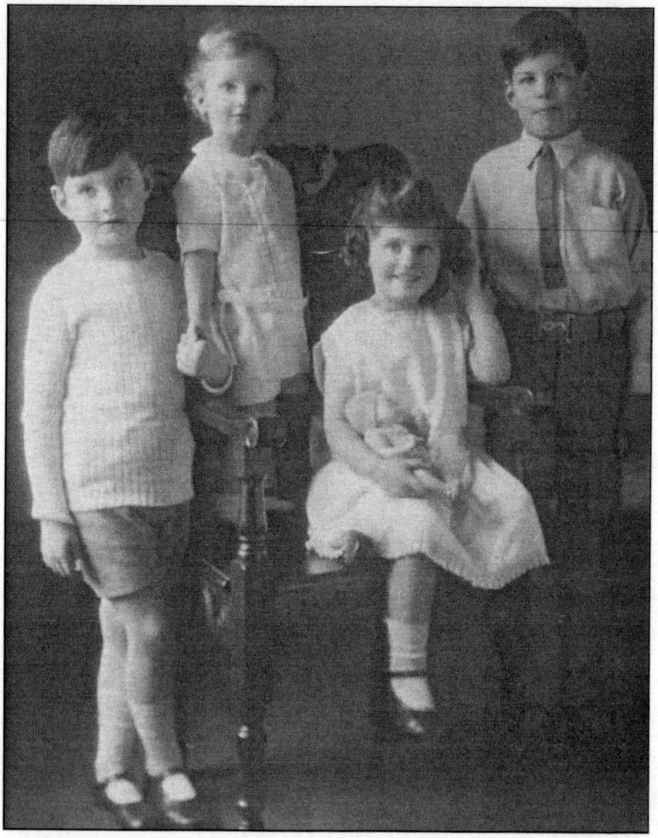

Philippa seated at Elmore Court with little brother John standing behind her, and first cousins David (left) and Mike Beaman (right), the sons of Sir Anselm's sister, Di.

special shed at the church for the car to be parked.

In the house there were about nine "domestics", starting with the cook, Mrs Cook, whose name sounds too convenient to be true; but Bertha Cook – from Berkeley just down the road – really was her name. Mrs Cook had a kitchen maid, although I better remember the scullery maid, Vianna, who peeled the vegetables and plucked the poultry in the large scullery room behind the kitchen. There was also a cold room facing north, as fridges then were rare things in country houses.

My mother would go down to the kitchen at 10 every morning to discuss the menu with Mrs Cook and write it all down on a slate. Mrs Cook kept chickens and every year raised a turkey for Christmas. One great excitement of our childhood was when, several weeks before Christmas, we were allowed into the kitchen to stir the Christmas pudding and watch as Mrs Cook put in several threepenny bits.

Louisa, our German Jewish parlour maid, wore a special uniform and waited at table. There was the housemaid who did the bedrooms. And then there was the "tweenie", who was at everyone's beck and call. All these staff had a servants' hall where they ate, and we children were never allowed in there! We had Nanny, and Nanny had a nursery maid called Doris. We all ate upstairs in the nursery and poor Doris had to carry all the food and drink up four flights of stairs.

In the garden were the fittingly named Mr Greenaway and his helper Tom. The grass was mown by a pony that pulled the lawnmower and wore leather boots so as not to mark the lawn. And then there was Mr Milliard who ran the estate for my father. Elmore was also home to Coldrick, who had looked after the horses and was now also the chauffeur. Though he was stone deaf it was Coldrick who taught me to ride. In the cold November mornings when the huntsmen, hounds and followers met at the gates at the end of Elmore Court drive, Coldrick on his horse Tommy and I on my black Welsh pony Ebony would join them and follow the hounds, with me firmly on a leading rein held by Coldrick beside me.

Before the War both my Grannies lived at Elmore Court. Granny Grant,[3] my

---

[3] Nina Frances Kennard – Granny Grant to be – was the second of four children of the Kennards of Eaton Place, Belgravia, with Irish family on her mother's side. In 1896, Nina had been an eligible 27-year-old brought over from the safety of Ireland to London to find and marry a titled young man. Instead she fell in love with an unknown 29-year-old adventurer from the north of Scotland called James Augustus Grant (that is, Grampapa, 1867-1932). After Oxford, James had worked in South Africa as a surveyor on the construction of the Kimberley-Bechuanaland Railway; in the service of the railway, had accompanied fellow Scot Joseph Thomson on his last expedition to the upper Congo in 1890; and had become

mother's mother, slept in the porch room (which was over the main porch), with a little room leading off it, called the dressing room, where normally the lady's husband would go to dress. But as a widow, Granny Grant had her lady's maid Ada in there instead. Granny Guise also had a lady's maid, Mrs Finch, who came up from the village every day. As her own sitting room Granny Grant had the morning room, so-called because it was always brightened by the morning sun.

There was also the smoking room where the men would smoke having donned

---

involved in Cecil Rhodes' plans for Central Africa. Thomson had written of the 23-year-old James: "a magnificent brawny fellow bronzed and bearded almost beyond recognition." But back in London and aged nearly 30 his only claim to fame had been that he was the oldest son of James Augustus Grant (1827-1892) who had been the partner of John Hanning Speke on the 1862 expedition to find the source of the Nile. When Nina met James in 1896 she was absolutely forbidden to marry him, so they eloped. She ran from the house in Eaton Place to where he was waiting in a hansom cab and they galloped to Brighton and were married. The Kennards at last deemed him acceptable when, having been Conservative Party Member of Parliament for Egremont (1910-1918), Whitehaven (1918-1922) and South Derbyshire (1924-1929), he was created 1st Baronet of Househill, Nairn, in 1926, and Nina became Lady Grant. In 1926 also their granddaughter Philippa was born. Years later, expecting to be given a catalogue of Grampapa James' achievements, Philippa asked her own mother (James' daughter Margaret) why he had been given a baronetcy, only to be told that he must have had many friends with great influence!

their very smart dark-green or purple-velvet smoking jackets. And beside the side door to the house was another important room, the gun room.

Ursula Wise, Philippa and Fräulein Weiss with Lady Guise's pet cockatoo on the Elmore lawn.

On 3 September 1939, war was declared. Our beloved Fräulein was not at Elmore that day, having gone for the summer holidays to her home in Münich, fully expecting to be back with us for the autumn term after the harvest was in. She had left all her clothes with us (which we were to send back to her after the war), and we wrote letters; I still have hers.[4]

[4] The text of a post-war letter from Fräulein Weiss, declining Philippa's invitation to her wedding, is included on page 129.

When war broke out I was with my family in the north of Scotland, one-and-a-half miles outside Nairn, at Granny Grant's house called Househill, which Grampapa had inherited from his father, the explorer James Augustus Grant. The "Granny" of my diaries, therefore, refers mainly (though not always) to Granny Grant. Every August while Granny Guise stayed at Elmore, my mother, father and brothers and I would go north with Granny Grant to Househill; and

Househill, Nairn.

packing to leave Elmore in 1939, so soon after we had waved to the Zeppelin, had seemed no different to us children. But having arrived at Househill in that August of

1939 we were not to go home to Elmore as a family for the whole duration of the war. Nairn was thought far safer for us children than the south of England. My diary entry for September 3rd, 1939, includes the lone word, "Speeches." The most famous and saddest of that day was by Prime Minister Neville Chamberlain, broadcast by the BBC only 15 minutes after the deadline that we had set for Hitler to agree a troop withdrawal from Poland. These are the still dreadful words that all Britain heard Mr Chamberlain say:

This morning the British Ambassador in Berlin handed the German Government a final Note stating that, unless we heard from them by 11 o'clock that they were prepared at once to withdraw their troops from Poland, a state of war would exist between us. I have to tell you now that no such undertaking has been received, and that consequently this country is at war with Germany.

In Scotland we were to have two further governesses, Miss Bamford from England and Mademoiselle Magron who was French Swiss, whom we did not like, and who we called "The Maggot"! My brothers had gone away to boarding school, so I shared the governesses with three friends, Ursula Wise, Mary Grant and Anne Murray. These three came from nearby but moved in to live with us at Househill for the sake of their education under our shared governess. Between us, we had two bedrooms, four ponies (Ebony among them, brought up from Elmore), and a lot of fun together at Househill.

Throughout the war each day I wrote a page in my diary about many everyday things, but now I am surprised by how much I wrote about the War. The diary was written with a fountain pen; the newly patented biros were not yet for sale!

Peace would come in 1945 when we went back to live at Elmore, but six years of war had made it a very different life. My mother could afford to employ just one domestic, Josepha, who was marvellous, and who came to Elmore from Spain with her husband Angel – he found work in a rope factory in Gloucester. But money was very tight and rationing was to go on until 1954. I married in 1950 when I had to stockpile a heap of ration coupons to get my trousseau together, not least my wedding dress and going-away outfit.

In fact everyone was poverty stricken until Margaret Thatcher came to power and then miraculously people began to earn "telephone numbers" in their pay packets. But that's another diary . . .

¤

2

The War Diary: aged 13

1939

Househill, Nairn.

September 1st
War is almost declared with Poland and Germany. Played golf with Mary Grant.

September 3rd
Sunday. War at 11 a.m. France and England fight Germany. Speeches. Granny cried. Went and picked sphagnum moss on the moors as dressings for the wounded.

UNITED

THE KING'S PLEA FOR JUSTICE AND FREEDOM

"Stand calm and firm and united," said his Majesty the King in a broadcast to the Empire last night.

The King's voice rose a little, and his pace increased when he spoke of meeting the challenge of a principle which, if it prevailed, would be fatal to the civilised order in the world. He again laid emphasis on the passage declaring that this principle, if established, would place the whole British Commonwealth of Nations in danger.

"The firmness of his voice increased when he said, "We can only do the right as we see the right."

The King spoke to his people from his study at Buckingham Palace. He wore the dark blue undress unifnrm of an Admiral of the Fleet.

His Majesty the King in the uniform of an Admiral of the Fleet. The King wore naval uniform when he broadcast to the Empire yesterday.

On the day Britain declared war, King George VI broadcast from Buckingham Palace to his subjects in Britain and the Commonwealth.

Parliamentary Report

Press Cuttings. The Press & Journal" Sept. 4th 1939.

FATEFUL SESSIONS OF PARLIAMENT

Mr Chamberlain on Collapse into Ruins of All He Had Worked for

NO GROUND FOR DOUBTS IN REGARD TO BRITAIN AND HER PLEDGE

"I Trust I may Live to See Hitlerism Destroyed"

HOUSE OF COMMONS

SUNDAY, September 3

Of the momentous statements which Mr CHAMBERLAIN has made to the House of Commons during the last few days, that which he made to a packed House to-day surpassed all.

The Deputy Leader of the Opposition referred to the atmosphere of anger and apprehension which reigned in the House yesterday. To-day the atmosphere is so happily changed. Yet underneath those two phases of mood is the reality of our determination to see this thing through.

The Deputy Leader of the Opposition has paid eloquent tribute to the restraint with which Poland has behaved during these last

hatred fires that were bound to arise. He also wanted to ask that the Prime Minister and the Government should again consider the question of aerial warfare, and whether even now it would not be possible to make a proposal to Germany and the world that we would be perfectly willing to abolish now aerial warfare in its entirety.

I have just come in from an air raid shelter after the warning, he added. What struck me was the calmness and the feeling that the Government and the country were in the right.

I know there was also underlying it the feeling that it is a terrible thing that either young people or old people should have lived to see the day when these foul weapons are being used.

He hoped that out of this there would arise a real spirit, a spirit that would compel people to give up reliance on force. Perhaps, this time, humanity would learn a lesson and refuse in the future to put its trust in poison gas, in the massacre of little children, and in universal hatred.

If mankind was to live in freedom and peace, there was only one way in which it could do so, and that was by a complete change of mind and outlook to enable us to see ourselves in other people and God in everybody.

MR LLOYD GEORGE

Britain Will Again Win a Victory for Right

Mr LLOYD GEORGE (Lib., Carnarvon Boroughs)—I am one of those who, from time to time, have challenged the handling of foreign affairs by the Government, but this is a different matter.

The Government are now confronted with the latest, but, I am afraid, not the last, of a series of acts of brigandage by a very formidable military Power which, if they are left unchallenged, will undermine the whole foundations of civilisation.

Philippa's own cutting from the *Aberdeen Press & Journal* 4 September 1939.

1940

January 11th

The war is going slowly on. Nobody seems to understand it. Poor Finland is now making a brave stand against silly Russia.[5] The

[5] World War Two was never a clear fight between the Allies and the Axis and, at first, much of the fighting did defy the British understanding of European affairs. The so-called Winter War between the Soviet Union and Finland began when the Communists invaded democratic republican Finland on November 30th, 1939. Finland had been part of the Czarist Russian Empire until the 1917 Bolshevik Revolution, and Soviet leader Joseph Stalin had seen the outbreak of war in September as a chance to reclaim lost territory, under the expedient of fortifying a buffer state against any German attack upon Leningrad through Scandinavia. There was some measure of Finno-Soviet peace from March 13th, 1940, to June 25th, 1941, but

U Boats are sinking a few of our ships. On the whole we are getting the best of it.

January 15th

I am knitting a pair of socks for the army, the first I have knitted.

January 20th

The coldest winter they have ever had in Europe.[6] We tobogganed down the shortcut.

The Severn frozen over at Elmore Back in January, 1940.

---

thereafter the two states were engaged in what is known as the Continuation War until September 19th, 1944.

[6] Winter 1939/40 was the coldest for 45 years. The Severn, Thames and other great rivers froze when temperatures plummeted especially on the night of January 23rd.

January 24th

At Elmore they have had 27°F of frost in the garden. The most we have had here is 24°.[7] The Severn is frozen across so that you can walk on it. John is knitting a scarf for the troops. There has been a great traffic hold up all over the British Isles because of the snow. No letters from the South.

"The service rendered by Finland to mankind is magnificent."

—Mr. WINSTON CHURCHILL

THE

FINLAND FUND

Has now received contributions in cash amounting to a total of

£115,000

which includes special donations to the Finnish Red Cross, sums received from the Special Appeal by the Paper Trade Committee organised by Mr. Wm. C. Corke and the Special Appeal to the Milling Industry organised by Sir Norman Vernon, and amounts collected by the Finnish Consuls and Vice-Consuls in Birmingham, Bradford, Cardiff, Dundee, Edinburgh, Falmouth, Hull, Jersey, Leeds, Liverpool, Manchester, Newport (Mon.), Preston and Weymouth.

Numerous gifts of jewelry, gold and silver objects, furs, clothing, soap and other supplies, many of them from anonymous donors, have also been gratefully received.

Hon. President: H.E. THE FINNISH MINISTER.

President: THE EARL OF PLYMOUTH, P.C.

Hon. Vice-President: H.E. MADAME GRIPENBERG.

Vice-Presidents: THE ARCHBISHOP OF CANTERBURY

THE EARL OF DERBY, K.G., P.C., G.C.B., G.C.V.O. THE EARL BEAUCHAMP.

THE LORD SNELL, P.C., C.B.E. LT.-GEN. SIR GEORGE MACDONOGH, G.B.E., K.C.B., K.C.M.G.

Hon. Treasurer: G. L. D'ABO, ESQ.

Council:

THE DUKE OF BUCCLEUCH, P.C., G.C.V.O.	SIR P. MALCOLM STEWART, BT.
THE VISCOUNT CRANBORNE, M.P.	SIR ALAN ANDERSON, G.B.E., M.P.
THE VISCOUNT BEARSTED, M.C.	SIR ROWLAND SPERLING, K.C.M.G., C.B.
THE BISHOP OF WINCHESTER.	MAJOR-GENERAL SIR WALTER MAXWELL SCOTT, C.B., D.S.O.
RT. REV. DAVID MATHEW (*Bishop Auxiliary of Westminster*).	LADY WEIGALL.
THE LORD DE SAUMAREZ.	R. O. HAMBRO, ESQ.
THE LORD WARDINGTON.	H. M. BELL, ESQ., C.V.O., C.B.E.
THE LORD PERRY, K.B.E.	LT.-COLONEL GEORGE CROSFIELD, C.B.E., D.S.O.
THE DEAN OF WESTMINSTER.	WM. C. CORKE, ESQ.
REV. ARCHIBALD MAIN, D.D., D.LIT. (*Moderator of the Church of Scotland*).	NORMAN BOHN, ESQ.
REV. ROBERT BOND, D.D.	A. C. BOSSOM, ESQ., M.P.
(*Moderator of the Federal Council of the Free Churches*).	PAUL CADBURY, ESQ.
	OSSIAN DONNER, ESQ.
THE CHIEF RABBI.	LEONARD ARNOTT, ESQ.

LIEUT.-COMMISSIONER ALFRED H. BARNETT (*of the Salvation Army*).

Executive Committee: THE LORD PHILLIMORE, M.C. THE DEAN OF ST. PAUL'S. SIR EDWARD REID, BT. SIR W. NORMAN VERNON, BT. DR. TANCRED BORENIUS, PH.D., D.LIT. MRS. AYRTON GOULD (*Chairman of the Labour Party*). W. HOLMES, ESQ. (*Chairman of the Trades Union Congress*). H. R. A. GARNETT, ESQ.

Secretary: J. F. LANDON, ESQ.

Hon. Auditors: MESSRS. THOMSON MCLINTOCK & CO.

Representative in Finland: H. M. BELL, ESQ., C.V.O., C.B.E.

In addition to a generous donation from H.R.H. The Princess Royal and Lord Harewood, the following contributions are gratefully acknowledged:—

From *The Times* February 1st, 1940.

[7] -27 Fahrenheit = -33 Celsius. -24 Fahrenheit = -31 Celsius.

1940 **February 1st**

The money problems are getting increasingly difficult with war going on. We children are not supposed to know anything about it, but we do. Wish I could do something.

February 2nd

Mummy has given Mackenzie, the parlour maid, the sack. So now we are going to economize and only have 5 maids. Jolly good thing too! The war is going slowly on, gallant little Finland still holding out. Polish people and all Jews in the Nazi grasp being killed off. Ships being sunk. All quiet on the Western Front. We have petrol rationing and only 4oz of butter each per week.

February 10th

Went to the cinema. Saw George Formby. He is very funny in *Keep Your Seats, Please*. We had the news film, a talk on America. So sorry to miss the Girl Guides.

February 17th

Brave little Finland is still gallantly holding out against big bully Russia.

March 13th

Gallant Finland has been forced to sign a peace treaty with Russia after 3 months of fighting over-powering numbers. We live in a sort of atmosphere of winning the War, that it would be an awful blow if we did not.

March 14th

The first civilian was killed on the Orkneys. Others were injured. They are the first on British soil since the War began.[8] Went to Girl Guides, we had to come back early because as Mum expressed it, "The soldiers might become rather familiar on the way home". We took our butter out to tea with us. We had gas-mask practice.

April 1st

Went to Daddy's office where he does a voluntary service thing with aeroplanes. It seems to be desperately secret.[9]

---

[8] The first British civilian to be killed in World War Two was 27-year-old Orcadian James Isbister, who died in his home settlement of Brig O'Waithe when 14 Junkers-88 Luftwaffe bombers (having raided Royal Navy warships in Scapa Flow) dropped their remaining bombs inland. Other histories date this event to March 16th, 1940.

[9] In the aftermath of bombs falling on Brig O'Waithe, it may be that Sir Anselm joined the Observation Corps (OC) of volunteers who, issued with Royal Navy binoculars, watched the skies for incoming enemy aircraft. Members had metal helmets and armbands, each bearing the OC initials. Their stations were often enough makeshift sheds nearby telegraph poles from which they could send alerts to a control centre. By July 3rd, however, Sir Anselm had certainly joined another group, the Local Defence Volunteers.

1940 **April 9th**

Hitler has invaded Norway and Denmark.[10] The latter has surrendered. Believed to be a sea battle going on.[11] It came with a dreadful crash on everyone. Goering and Goebbels and the rest say they did it to protect the neutrals from invasion by Britain. All the five wirelesses go blaring on every hour. I am selfish. I just want everything to happen to help Britain though. Very sorry for Denmark and Norway.

---

[10] The British and French had been openly proposing that they should occupy Norway but in the early hours of April 9th Germany invaded both Norway and Denmark in Operation *Weserübung*, ostensibly to protect the two countries' neutrality against Allied invasion. Denmark had signed a 10-year non-aggression pact with Germany in 1939. Germany's invasion of Denmark on April 9th met only two hours of military resistance before the Danish government surrendered. (German-Danish economic co-operation went on until 1943 when Denmark refused further co-operation and scuttled most of its navy, sending as many officers as they could to Sweden.) Operation *Weserübung* was over by June 10th with complete German victory also in Norway, and marking the end of the beginning of the Norwegian Campaign by the Allies to wrest mastery of Scandinavia from the Axis.

[11] The first engagements of the Norwegian Campaign were the Battles of Narvik from April 9th to June 8th – on water in Ofotfjord and in the hills about Narvik city. The two naval battles in the Ofotfjord on April 10th and 13th were fought between the British and German navies, while the two-month land campaign was fought by Norwegian, French, British and Polish troops against German troops, shipwrecked sailors and paratroops. On April 10th in Ofotfjord both navies sank two of their enemies' destroyers, Germany also losing one ammunition supply ship and six cargo ships to the Royal Navy guns.

April 11th

We seem to have sunk the German Navy.

April 13th

Aunt Bunny[12] came to stay from London. She has got a censor's job. We have sunk quite a few German ships and landed some troops at Narvik.[13] Good news.

April 17th

Had my German lesson with Louisa who is very depressed with Hitler etc. Louisa is a German Jewess, who came as parlour maid, as a refugee. All her relatives had disappeared in concentration camps.

May 10th

The Germans have gone into both Holland and Belgium.[14] Just like that, they say they

---

[12] Philippa's mother's sister, Hester Renton.

[13] On April 13th the Second Naval Battle of Narvik saw no British ships lost, but heavy German losses: eight destroyers sunk or scuttled and one U-boat sunk.

[14] During the late evening of May 9th, German forces occupied Luxembourg. That night German troops entered the Netherlands and Belgium. On the morning of May 10th, German paratroopers landed in the Netherlands at The Hague, and elsewhere in both the Netherlands and Belgium to open the way for German troops. This assault on the Low Countries was the start of the Battle of France in which, by the end of May, the British Expeditionary Force had been pushed to evacuate with several French divisions from Dunkirk. On June 22nd an armistice would be signed by France and Germany to show that France had fallen and was thence under German occupation in the north and west, under Italian occupation in the

1940 are protecting them against us. They have dropped 4 incendiary bombs in Kent.

May 15th

This evening Louisa was giving us our German lesson, when Dad came in with a telegram. Holland has fallen today.[15] Germans overran it. She went deadly pale. She was told to ring up London. She is so excitable. She cries more than she laughs.

May 17th

Went off to be victims for the ARP people to practice on.[16]

---

southeast, while central and southern France was "free" under the Vichy Government.

[15] German-Jewish Louisa had sisters in Amsterdam (the Netherlands) and Brussels (Belgium). Germany had invaded the Low Countries on May 9th. After Germany's aerial bombing of Netherlandish Rotterdam on May 14th, and with their French allies failing to halt the German advance, that same evening the armies of the Netherlands surrendered. The capitulation document was signed on May 15th.

[16] Air Raid Precautions (ARP) was an organisation set up in the United Kingdom in 1924, as a response to the fears about the growing threat from the development of bomber aircraft, dedicated to the protection of civilians from the danger of air-raids. Air Raid wardens or ARP wardens had the task of patrolling the streets during blackout, to ensure that no light was visible. ARP wardens were trained in basic fire-fighting and first aid, and could keep an emergency situation under control until official rescue services arrived.

May 21st

The Germans are in France, Amiens, we have driven them out of Arras. Ursula and I went down to the beach and talked a lot.

May 22nd

Elmore is to be let. All sorts of people want it, but Granny Guise has telephoned to say, can the Aunts at Lintonfield[17] and the Wentworths[18] go there? Mummy said, "Could the Belgian refugees have the kitchen area?" Two hours later a telegram came saying, could Princess Juliana and Queen Wilhelmina of Holland go there?[19] Dad said "Yes". The telephone is so bad. Well, when the telegram came Dad was in Inverness and Mum in Nairn. So I bicycled to Nairn with the telegram. I felt very important. The Germans are in Boulogne. I feel absolutely sick with excitement, the

---

[17] Sir Anselm Guise's maiden aunts Marnie, Lily and Georgie, who lived at Lintonfield house near Bristol.

[18] The Wentworths were cousins in London.

[19] An evacuation to the United Kingdom of the Netherlands royal family had been planned since at least the end of 1939. Netherlandish Queen Wilhelmina (widowed in 1934) and her only child Princess Juliana fled The Hague, boarded a British destroyer and retreated to England. The Netherlands armed forces, apart from those in Zeeland, had surrendered on 15 May 1940. In Britain, Queen Wilhelmina took charge of the Netherland Government in exile. In fact, Queen Wilhelmina did not take Elmore Court but found another house to live in, and Philippa's home was taken by the Admiralty, which, however, it never occupied.

telephone rings all day. We all stayed up and listened to the King. He spoke awfully well. Hardly stuttered once.

May 29th

We, the Allies, have taken Narvik, at last. We are having an awful time in Belgium, and we have started to evacuate. These Germans machine gun any living thing they can see, refugees and civilians. Every day someone seems to die, who Mum and Granny know. It is an awful feeling when you hear someone is dead and gone forever.

June 1st

The Polish Scouts refused to obey the Germans, so they were lined up and the Germans shot them down while they were singing *Long Live Poland*.[20] We went for a bathe and had a picnic. It was so lovely, so carefree, no war.

June 3rd

Anne got a letter from her sister, which had to go through the censors. She wanted to

---

[20] On September 3rd, 1939, two days after the start of the German invasion of Poland, took place the "Bloody Sunday" massacre of many, maybe hundreds, of ethnic German citizens in and about the Polish city of Bydgoszcz. In reprisal the occupying German army killed hundreds of Poles including some Boy Scouts who were lined up against a wall in Bydgoszcz marketplace and shot. It is likely this massacre of which Girl Guide Philippa has heard some nine months on.

write she had seen a sea-plane, so she wrote she had seen a winged sea monster, grey in colour, and it was dropping bombs.

June 4th

The evacuation of Dunkirk, a flotilla of little boats from the south coast crossed the Channel and helped to bring back off the beaches of Dunkirk our retreating troops. Wonderful.[21]

3

The War Diary: aged 14

June 10th

My birthday. I am 14. Italy has come into the war with Germany.[22]

June 17th

France has asked for peace terms. We suppose she will give in.

---

[21] See footnote to May 10th, 1940.

[22] Although an Axis ally, Fascist Italy had been non-belligerent until June 10th, 1940. On that day in the Battle of France the German invasion pushed the French Government from Paris to Bordeaux. Sensing France would soon fall, Mussolini swiftly declared war on France and Britain.

1940 **June 24th**

The French have given up fighting and signed some shameful treaty with Germany and Italy. Italy has not done a thing yet, except unsuccessful raids in Africa. The French Colonies are going on.

June 28th

Syria has gone over to the Germans.[23] The Russians have taken Basarabi in Rumania.[24] I have now got completely reconciled to bad news, but have complete confidence in our

---

[23] Syria and Lebanon were with Germany in that they were controlled by Vichy France. Between July 8th and June 14th the Allies successfully fought the Syria–Lebanon campaign, which ended with those lands coming under Free French rule.

[24] Neutral Romania had sought guarantees from Hitler that no territory would be lost in the worsening European wars, not knowing of the secret protocol in the 1939 non-aggression Molotov-Ribbentrop Pact, by which the USSR and Germany had agreed to split eastern Europe into spheres of influence. Romania fell into the Soviet sphere so Hitler was in no position to honour any assurance he might offer against Russian territorial claims. On June 26th (four days after Romania's former territorial guarantor, France, had capitulated to Germany), the USSR demanded the Romanian Government withdraw from the regions of Bessarabia, Northern Bukovina and Hertza. Within hours of Moscow's threat of war Romania had agreed, and the Red Army's occupation was complete within six days. Bessarabia may have been misunderstood by young Philippa as Basarabi (now called Murfatlar) in Romania's Black Sea jurisdiction of Constanța, some 80 miles south of Bessarabia (which is itself now split between Moldova and Ukraine).

winning in the end. I think this is because of Churchill's stirring speeches.

July 3rd

The telephone went and asked for Daddy to go immediately to his LDV post.[25] There are millions of aeroplanes flying everywhere. The Germans may have landed. We are not allowed to go out of the gates.

July 4th

We have got the French navy.[26] We just took it. This is the best thing we have done since the war began. We went to see Deana Durbin in *First Love*. It was excellent. She sings awfully well. We had a good newsreel. We gathered sphagnum moss. It is an antiseptic, and is used instead of cotton wool, for the wounded.

July 12th

Mr. Walls, the dentist, told us that four high-explosive bombs were dropped at Moy,

---

[25] The LDV (Local Defence Volunteers) had been inaugurated in a radio broadcast of 14 May 1940, in which Secretary of State for War Anthony Eden called on all willing men aged 17 to 65 to sign up as members of this putative militia. Created to arm and train the British population to resist a German invasion, the LDV was to be renamed as the Home Guard from 22 July 1940.

[26] On July 3rd, 1940, the Royal Navy bombarded and sank the Vichy fleet at its base at Mers-el-Kébir on the coast of what was then French Algeria, even though Vichy France was not a belligerent power.

near Inverness, by German airplanes. The noise they make is 20 ticks, then miss 3 tick-beats, and so on.[27]

At the lone shed standing on the Old Bar. From left to right, Philippa, Ursula and Mum, with the dogs Deb and Ben.

July 15th

All the windows are covered with crisscross bomb-resistant tape to stop the glass flying about. Enormous posts i.e. tree trunks are being erected on the sands going out to the Old Bar to prevent the German aeroplanes landing.[28]

---

[27] From July to the end of October, 1940, was waged the Battle of Britain in which Germany tried to win air superiority, and to bomb British shipping convoys and ports, and force the UK to surrender by terror bombing of civilian targets. Britain did not surrender its skies and the German plan to invade Britain by sea and air was scuppered.

[28] The Old Bar is a spit of sand and shingle, less than five metres high, to the east of Nairn, curving southwest for nearly three miles. It was feared that at low tide the sand

July 23rd

Russia has taken Latvia and all the states round there.[29] We have a new budget: 8s 6d in the £ (Super tax).[30] Half the people say it is not hard enough. A funny state of affairs. It was expected to be 10/- in the £.[31] We seem to live much the same as before, though everyone talks of the dreadful poverty to come. Mummy says she would rather have no maids and something to spend.

July 29th

Our Air Force is doing marvellously well. We seem to shoot down most of the Germans and not lose any of our air-craft.

---

and mud between the Old Bar and the shore would be firm enough for aircraft to land.

[29] Under the 1939 Molotov Ribbentrop Pact's secret protocol Germany had surrendered Latvia, Finland and Estonia to the Soviet sphere of influence. The USSR had pushed Latvia to garrison from October 1939 up to 30,000 Red Army troops but, on June 17th, 1940, this "mutual assistance" turned into an unopposed Soviet invasion. By August 5th, 1940, Soviet deportation and murder of Latvians, and rigging of elections, had transformed the former nationalist dictatorship into the Latvian Soviet Socialist Republic.

[30] That is in decimal terms, 42.5 pence in the pound. On June 23rd Chancellor of the Exchequer Sir Kingsley Wood announced the third War Budget, with the income tax rise noted by Philippa, beer up 1d a pint, and a purchase tax introduced for first time at 33% on luxuries.

[31] That is, 50 pence in the decimal pound.

1940 Cousin Frank Guise[32] picked up two young German pilots, who had parachuted down, after their plane was shot down. He said they were very frightened.

August 13th

Our air force is a wonder. We English are proud to be fighting half Europe alone.

August 17th

Hitler said on 15th August he would dine at Buckingham Palace. Instead we brought down 167 German planes with a loss of only 20 on our side.

August 27th

Eastington has been bombed. The Bush's place in Gloucestershire.[33] Eight bombs have been dropped on a farm at Elmore Back.[34]

---

[32] Francis Edward Boissier Guise (1892-1970) was a great-grandson of General Sir John Wright Guise, 3rd Bt, as was Philippa's father Sir Anselm William Edward Guise, 6th Bt (1888-1970).

[33] Eastington village in Gloucestershire is some eight miles south of Elmore. Eastington Park, to the east of the village church, was the grand home of Claude de Lisle Bush and his family. A World War One veteran, Claude was to die on January 22nd, 1941, aged 47, while a lieutenant with the 3rd Battalion Gloucestershire Regiment. A letter from Claude de Lisle Bush to Philippa, dated January 3rd, 1940, can be found on p.134.

[34] Elmore Back on the Severn is some two miles north of Elmore.

September 3rd
We have now been at war for a year. It does not seem as long and is certainly quite different to what we thought it would be like.

September 5th
London is having bad air-raids. One day 300 people killed and 1,000 seriously injured. They raided the Docks.[35]

September 6th
A new war table:
12 pence = 1 shilling
20 shilling = £1
£50,000 = 1 Spitfire
1 Spitfire = 30 Messerschmitts

[35] After the sunset of August 24th, 1940, and in the thick of the Battle of Britain, German bombers had drifted from their intended military targets on London's outskirts. Instead they mistakenly dropped their bombs inside London, destroying several homes and killing civilians. The British Government answered public outrage with retaliatory bombing of Germany's capital the next night. Within the week British bombers had hit Berlin three times, not least to goad the Germans to turning their firepower from R.A.F. airfields and on to British cities. Philippa's diary entry shows the Luftwaffe still targeting industrial and military targets. But within two days this had changed. From September 7th, and for 57 consecutive nights Londoners were bombed in their homes, and often thereafter until May 21st, 1941, by which date several other big British towns had been likewise heavily bombarded.

1940 **September 7th**

We shot down 104 German planes for 15 of our own.[36]

Philippa's Dad, Sir Anselm Guise, in his Home Guard uniform.

[36] First day of the Blitz.

September 8th

Went to church. Today is being held as a day of national prayer by special request of the King. The church was packed, but there was a scare, so all the Home Guard and the soldiers were out on duty all over Britain.

September 15th

We shot down 185 German planes today, only losing 25 of our own.[37]

September 27th

The Germans have sunk an evacuee ship going to America. It carried 100 children. 76 drowned. Awful.[38]

---

[37] On Sunday, September 15th, the Luftwaffe launched its fiercest attack against London in the hope of drawing out the R.A.F. into a battle of annihilation. Around 1,500 aircraft took part in the dogfights that raged until sundown. This was the climax of the Battle of Britain and, ever since, September 15th has been kept as Battle of Britain Day. Philippa quotes the Air Ministry's immediate statement of between 175 and 185 German "kills", three times the true number. The claim of 25 downed R.A.F. fighters was nearer the mark, the total being 29.

[38] Over six days in September the German submarine U-48 sank eight ships from two convoys. One of those ships was, after sunset on September 18th, SS City of Benares, a refugee ship bearing about 100 children from Blitz-stricken Britain to safety in Canada. Most of the 258 dead, 77 of them children, died from exposure in the water, or were drowned. Some of the 148 survivors were picked up only after having spent eight days in a lifeboat. The sinking ended the Children's Overseas Reception Board evacuation programme.

1940 **October 8th**

The Duchess of Gloucester is staying with Lady Constance Cairns.[39] Today she inspected the hospital and the Guides and Brownies formed a guard of honour.[40] Of course, we three went. We were told to cheer her so we started off and no-one else did. It sounded so silly. We cheered a bit better when she left. She looked very smart in WAAF uniform. She had a detective and a lady-in-waiting. Everyone was in an awful flutter.

October 13th

Princess Elizabeth broadcast for the first time.[41] Very good. Very clear voice. She is the same age as me.

---

[39] From 1939 to October 4th, 1943, Princess Alice, Duchess of Gloucester, was the inaugural head of the Women's Auxiliary Air Force (WAAF). She was thereafter Director of the WAAF until August 1944. Lady Constance Cairns of Carnach House, Nairn, five-years the widow of the Hon Douglas Halyburton Cairns, was the daughter of William Henry Walter Montagu Douglas Scott, 6th Duke of Buccleuch and 8th Duke of Queensberry.

[40] Balblair House was Nairn's hospital and local authority nursing home.

[41] This a transcript of Princess Elizabeth's speech to children evacuated away from their families: "Thousands of you in this country have had to leave your homes and be separated from your fathers and mothers. My sister - Margaret Rose - and I feel so much for you, as we know from experience what it means to be away from those we love most of all. To you, living in new surroundings, we send a message of true sympathy; and at the same time

October 21st

Mrs Wise, Ursula's Mum, was machine-gunned in Dorset! She dived into a ditch and the German plane did not get her. Mr Winston Churchill spoke this evening to the French people, first in French and then in English.[42] Bad accent in French. The Germans tried to block the air-space.

October 27th

Three men landed in a rubber boat at the Old Bar, Nairn. The Old Bar is a spit of land running along the coast and when the tide is in it is cut off from the mainland. They said they had escaped from a German boat and were Norwegians. They were arrested under suspicion of being spies. We rode over to the Old Bar. We could not find a sign of the rubber boat.

October 28th

Greece is fighting Italy.[43] Aunt Tootoo's house in London has been bombed flat,[44]

---

we would like to thank the kind people who have welcomed you to their homes in the country."

[42] Only days away from being able to declare victory in the Battle of Britain, Churchill's speech, known as *Dieu Protégé la France*, included this dark wit: "Here in London, which Herr Hitler says he will reduce to ashes, and which his aeroplanes are now bombarding, our people are bearing up unflinchingly. Our Air Force has more than held its own. We are waiting for the long-promised invasion. So are the fishes."

[43] The Balkan Campaign began with this Greco-Italian War in which Italy invaded on October 28th. Greece was

churches and many other places too. It really is awful. Aunt Tootoo is coming to live here. She arrived very dilapidated having taken 2 days to come from Durham. About a fortnight ago on the wireless we heard a bomb fall during the reading of the news. Just heard that a woman was killed in the next-door room. Bruce Belfrage, the reader of the news, went on as usual.[45] Brave.

November 2nd

Some British soldiers have gone into Greece.

November 3rd

There was a practice of the siren. It is not as loud as people say. We then went to the Druim for a Halloween party.[46] We ducked for apples. So did the grown-ups. It was

---

repulsing the Italians until, on April 6th, 1941, Germany also invaded. Greece surrendered in the armistice of April 23rd, 1941.

[44] A first cousin of Philippa's Granny Grant, Aunt Tootoo was so-called because her mother had always said she was "too too beautiful!"

[45] English actor and newsreader Bruce Belfrage was 39 when, on October 15th, 1940, the BBC's Broadcasting House in Westminster took a direct hit from a delayed-action German bomb. The bomb then exploded as Belfrage read the 9pm news. Wireless listeners heard a dull thud, but seven were killed; and Belfrage, covered with plaster and soot, kept on news-reading as though nothing had happened.

[46] "The Druim" was the home of the Brodies, friends of Philippa's parents.

screamingly funny to see all their permed heads or bald ones coming out sopping wet.

November 5th
We had our first air-raid. The siren boomed out during dinner. Some bombs were dropped at Kingussie.

November 6th
Mr Roosevelt has got in again in the American Presidency election. He has broken all previous rules by entering for it the third time.[47]

November 10th
Mr Chamberlain has died.[48] I really do feel awfully sad.

November 13th
We have sunk half the Italian Navy.[49] Best piece of news we have had. Aunt Tootoo cried with joy. Urs got a letter from her

---

[47] Franklin Delano Roosevelt, President of the United States in his third term 1933–1945. The American convention of limiting Presidents to two terms was confirmed in the United States Constitution's 22nd Amendment in 1947.

[48] Neville Chamberlain had been Prime Minister until May 10th, 1940, when he was succeeded by Winston Churchill. Chamberlain died on November 9th, 1940.

[49] In the Battle of Taranto, on the night of November 11/12th, the British navy attacked the Italian navy as it lay at anchor in the harbour of Taranto. The sitting-duck Italians lost half their leading ships in the action, if not half the whole *Regia Marina*.

mother. She said that three of Eaton Place houses have gone and there is a time bomb at the end of the street. So 32 the corner house is still standing. I should not think it will do so for long.[50]

November 17th

Coventry has had the most awful bombing. We have retaliated by laying Hamburg flat.[51]

November 19th

Cousin Enid Nutting[52] told us that John Nutting, her son, has been drowned on a military scheme. Granny cried all through dinner. Cousin John was just engaged to be married. *So* sad.

---

[50] 32 Eaton Place, London, where Philippa was born, was Granny Grant's house. The house did in fact survive the London Blitz and Philippa's family went to live there after the war.

[51] Coventry was repeatedly hit by German bombing from August 1940, the worst raid being on November 14th, 1940. On the nights of November 15/16th and 16/17th more than 200 R.A.F. aircraft bombed Hamburg.

[52] The wife of Sir Harold Stansmore Nutting, 2nd Bt. of St Helens in Booterstown in the County of Dublin, Enid Nutting was a cousin of Granny Grant, and lived at Quenby Hall, Leicestershire. John Nutting's death aged 26 was to be followed by that of his younger brother Edward also at 26, also in action, in January 1943. Enid's youngest son lived to become Rt. Hon. Sir Harold Anthony Nutting, 3rd Bt.

November 28th

In the morning Pamela, Mary and I went to help at the canteen. I do so enjoy it. It is very funny to hear the soldiers at the counter saying, "A cup o' tea, ma'am." And then meeting us outside and saying, "'Ello, little girl!"

Nina Grant as a pretty young woman (above), and in later life at Househill, Nairn, as Lady Grant (right), the Granny whom Philippa knew.

December 5th

Urs, Pam and me went to the canteen. There was a terrible rush. One soldier came and asked me for a "plight". I couldn't think what he meant, and went and asked. And of course it turned out to be a "plate". I did feel such a fool! Another asked me for a "packet of water bugs". I went and asked, and it turned out to be a "packet of Woodbines"! [53] The Greeks are still doing fine, pushing the Italians back all the way through Albania.[54]

December 12th

The British in Africa had a marvellous victory over the Italians. Took Sidi Barrani.[55] We took at least 20 thousand Italian prisoners. Lots of equipment also. Done under General Wavell's command.[56] The Greeks still doing wonderfully well. In the morning I went to the canteen. Terrible rush. Told to make the tea "as sweet as myself" etc.

December 31st

The last day of an eventful year in history. Russia took Finland. Germany took Norway, Denmark, Holland, Belgium and France. There came the epic of Dunkirk. Then the awful air-raids on London and the marvellous victories of the R.A.F. Now we

---

[53] Woodbine was a brand of filterless cigarette.

[54] See footnote to October 28th, 1940.

[55] The Battle of Sidi Barrani, on Egypt's Mediterranean coast, on December 8th to 10th, 1940, was the first major Allied operation of the Western Desert Campaign and a decisive victory for Britain over Italian forces.

[56] Field Marshal Archibald Percival Wavell, 1st Earl Wavell.

have taken 38,000 Italian prisoners in the Western Desert. Also the Greeks are doing fine against the Italians in Albania beside many others such as the threat of invasion. A year full of experiences for myself, which has made me older. This morning ponies escaped, gate open. This afternoon went in and had our second diphtheria inoculation. Then we snowballed and tobogganed.

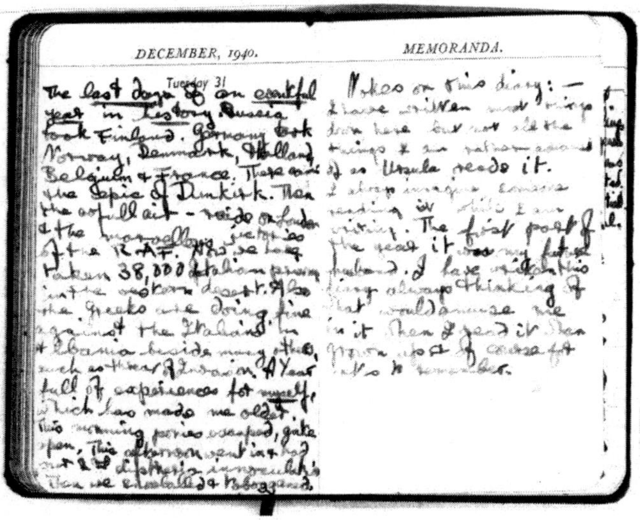

Notes on this diary: I have written most things down here, but not all the things I am rather ashamed of as Ursula reads it. I always imagine someone reading it while I am writing. The first part of the year it was my future husband. I have written this diary always thinking of what would amuse me in it when I read it when grown up[57] and of course for notes to remember.

---

[57] The author is now aged 87.

1941

January 1st

New Year's Day. I wonder what's ahead of us in the coming year. Mayhap invasion, victory or defeat and loss of life. This morning woke up to the country pure white, three inches of snow. I feel pretty frightful after diphtheria inoculation. New Year Resolutions: Must be reasonable and thoughtful to new governess.[58] Must not be contrary or jealous. Must not make such a noise. Must say prayers. Must keep the ponies and saddlery spick and span.

January 6th

Bardia[59] has fallen. We have taken 94,000 Italian prisoners (in the Western Desert). I am very sorry for silly old Muso but he is getting his desserts for being such a greedy jackal over France.[60] I am knitting my first jumper for the R.A.F.

---

[58] This was Miss Bamford. Philippa's last governess, Miss Magron, was to take over on May 2nd, 1941.

[59] Bardia or El Burdi is a Mediterranean seaport in eastern Libya, heavily fortified by the Italians. The town was taken during Operation Compass by Commonwealth forces consisting mainly of the Australian 6th Division in fighting over January 3rd to 5th, 1941.

[60] In the Franco-German armistice that ended the Battle of France on June 22nd, 1940, Italy under her Prime Minister (1922-43) Benito "Muso" Mussolini was awarded southeast France as a territorial concession.

January 7th

We have advanced on Tobruk.[61] I must say our forces in the East are doing well.

January 9th

Baden-Powell has died.[62] He was a great man. Great soldier in South Africa. The Chief Scout.

January 12th

The meat ration has been reduced to 1 shilling per head. Mum finds it very difficult to know what to give us to eat. I am reading *Jock of the Bushvelt* and *Wuthering Heights*.[63]

---

[61] Tobruk is a Mediterranean seaport in eastern Libya, heavily fortified in the War by the Italians. The town was to be taken by Allied forces, mainly the Australian 6th Division, on January 22nd, 1941

[62] Robert Baden-Powell served in the British Army from 1876 until 1910 in India and Africa. In 1899, during the Second Boer War in South Africa, Baden-Powell successfully defended the town in the Siege of Mafeking. In 1907, he held the first Brownsea Island Scout camp, which is now seen as the start of the Scouting movement. In 1920, the first World Scout Jamboree took place in Olympia in West Kensington, and Baden-Powell was acclaimed Chief Scout of the World.

[63] Food of another sort: *Jock of the Bushvelt* (1907) by Percy Fitzpatrick and *Wuthering Heights* (1847) by Emily Brontë.

1941 **January 15th**

Major Oldham promised us all a ride in the Bren Gun Carrier.[64] We all six got into the carrier with a soldier. We were allowed to steer in turn. We just roared over gorse bushes. The sand flew up in our faces. Went to P.E. The man who taught us has the hairiest chest I have ever seen. Jamie is quite good at P.E. We went to the cinema to see *The Blue Bird*, one of Shirley Temple's. She is a marvellous little girl. In the evening we heard London is on fire in the great Sunday night air raid. Also heard of streams of Italians taken prisoner in Libya.

January 20th

The Duchess of Kent broadcast an appeal for the WRNS.[65] Also listened to President Roosevelt.

---

[64] The Oldham family, like the Guises and several other families, were living in Nairn through the War. Major Oldham was serving in the Army. The Bren Gun Carrier was the nickname for the Universal Carrier, a light armoured vehicle on caterpillar tracks, built by Vickers-Armstrong between 1934 and 1960, and used widely by British Commonwealth forces during the War. Universal Carriers were usually used for transporting personnel and equipment, mostly support weapons, or as machine-gun platforms.

[65] Women's Royal Naval Service – the "Wrens" – was formed as the Royal Navy's women's branch in 1917, disbanded in 1919, and revived in 1939 (being integrated into the Royal Navy in 1993). Princess Marina of Greece and Denmark, the Duchess of Kent, was Commandant, and later Chief Commandant, from 1940 until her death in 1968.

January 23rd
Tobruk has fallen. We have taken some 20,000 Italian prisoners. Old Muso's army is rotten, or we are wonderful.

January 25th
In Libya, Abyssinia and Italian Somaliland the British are gradually capturing the last Italians, I think now about 140,000 so far. Hurrah for us! Germany seems to be trying to take some of the strain of Italy. The Italians are rioting. Fruit has become very short. In fact bananas are no longer being imported. There are very few oranges and we have eaten up all our apples and there are none to be got so instead we have prunes and grapefruit in the morning. Went to church forced to wear that ridiculous felt hat. In the afternoon we went down to the minister's pond and skated and played ice-hockey.

February 4th
The British are doing wonderfully well against the Italians on all fronts in Africa. The Greeks are doing the same in Albania.

February 8th
Benghazi has fallen.[66] That means Libya is ours. Our whole Army marched 150 miles in

---

[66] Benghazi in Libya was captured from the Italians by the Australian 6th Division on February 6th, 1941. The town

30 hours across the desert. Never has such a feat been done before. Hurrah for us!

February 20th

Aunt Tootoo told us that she watched the bell tower in St Marks Square, Venice, fall before the War,[67] only she never realised it because at that moment she was rather tipsy and when she could not see it she thought it confirmed she was tipsy!

February 24th

In the evening went to see *The Great Dictator*.[68] It is a wonderful film. Charlie Chaplin took two parts, one Hitler and two a Jewish barber. There was a meaning behind it all. Paulette Goddard, so pretty. He, Charlie Chaplin, made a most impassioned appeal for peace in concluding speech. The

---

was taken by Germany on April 4th, by Britain on December 24th, by the Germans again on January 29th, 1942, and at last by Britain on November 20th, 1942.

[67] St Mark's Campanile is the bell tower of St Mark's Basilica in Venice's Piazza San Marco. In July 1902, the north wall of the tower began to show signs of a dangerous crack that in the following days continued to grow. At last, on Monday, July 14th, around 9.45am, the Campanile collapsed completely. Aunt Tootoo must have had rather a boozy breakfast that morning.

[68] *The Great Dictator* (1940) written and directed by Charlie Chaplin, who also starred as the Hitler-like Adenoid Hynkel and as an amnesic Jewish Barber. The barber sees afresh the persecution of the Jews, and falls in love with the Jewish washerwoman, Hannah (Paulette Goddard).

whole film was so real. Ticked Hitler off well.

March 4th

Bulgaria has gone over to Germany.[69] I wish to goodness these Germans would have a rebuke. I am not going to eat so much. There is a war on. This funny one-eyed cook does cook well. We had an argument about the war, what we should feel if the Germans should arrive. I personally and Mary feel we would fight on the housetops, in the streets, and would never give into slavery, although Ursula more reasonably would act like Denmark etc does.[70]

March 6th

Daddy has come back from the South. One of the bomb craters in London has a bridge spanning it for traffic. Blast is a strange thing, the way it travels in one direction. Elmore is going on well. There are two large bomb craters on the top of Hockley Hill, at Elmore.[71]

---

[69] Previously neutral, in March 1941 Bulgaria formally signed the Tripartite Pact, becoming a German ally, and German troops entered the country in preparation for the German invasion of Greece and Yugoslavia.

[70] See footnote to April 9th, 1940.

[71] Hockley Hill is about one mile south of Elmore Court.

March 21st

My favourite poet is Tennyson, then Browning, then Wordsworth and John Masefield. I notice most of the soldiers seem to have false teeth, but none of them have glasses.

April 6th

Germany has declared war on Yugoslavia and gallant Greece.[72] We have taken the capital of Abyssinia Addis Ababa.[73] We have sunk most of the Italian navy.[74] Daddy goes Home Guarding every Sunday and Thursday.

April 10th

The Germans are advancing in Yugoslavia and Greece. Really I almost sweat to think of the gallant people being so ruthlessly conquered and to know that there is a possibility for that to happen to us. Washed my hair. In the morning went riding. On the way back on the Lochloy Road a good-looking young officer stepped out and asked

---

[72] See footnote to October 28th, 1940.

[73] Addis Ababa was liberated from the Italians on April 6th by forces under Lieutenant-General Alan Cunningham. Haile Selassie, Emperor of Ethiopia, had been exiled by the 1936 Italian conquest of Abyssinia, but would be restored to Addis Ababa by the British on May 5th, 1941.

[74] The Battle of the Tarigo Convoy was fought off the Kerkennah Islands of Tunisia on April 16th, 1941, between four British and three Italian destroyers. Britain lost one destroyer, Italy three destroyers and five cargo ships.

for the loan of our ponies. They were soldiers from Strathpeffer attacking Nairn. This young man on an exercise wanted to ride up the road to see where the enemy were. I went with him, he seemed a very resourceful young man.

April 19th

The news is very bad. We are losing Libya again to the Germans. Yugoslavia gone. Retreating in Greece.

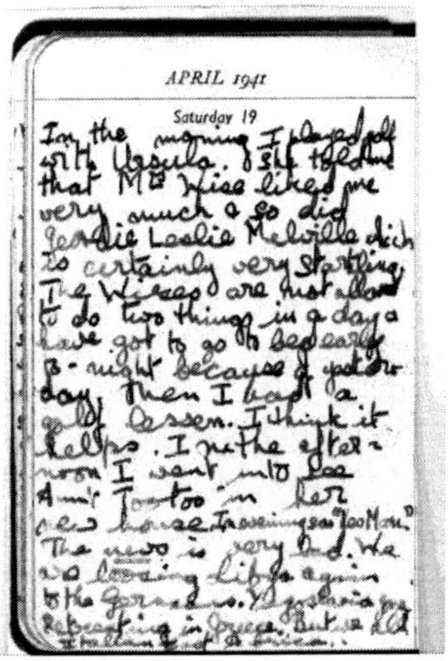

April 29th

Saw *Pride and Prejudice*. We saw a trailer for *Captains Courageous*. The song, the heart-pulling *Don't Cry, Little Fish, Don't Cry.*[75] Lord Leven gave Mum an 8lb salmon.[76]

---

[75] In the 1937 movie of Rudyard Kipling's novel *Captains Courageous* Spencer Tracey plays fisherman Manuel

May 2nd

Miss Magron, the new governess, arrived. She met us on the doorstep talking French.[77] We were flabbergasted. We all expected an old hag with a long nose. Instead rather a pretty youngish woman stood before us. We were speechless. She spoke French to Mum and Gran all lunch. In the afternoon took Ebony to the blacksmith.

May 27th

The Hood has been sunk, our biggest battleship. In fact the biggest in the world.[78]

Fidello who sings the song generally known as *Yea Ho, Little Fish*.

[76] Archibald Alexander Leslie-Melville, 13th Earl of Leven, 12th Earl of Melville (1890–1947) was Lord Lieutenant of Nairnshire from 1935 to 1947. In age-order his children were Jean, Sandy, Geordie, Ronald and Alan. The family seat is Glenferness House near Nairn.

[77] Miss Magron was French-Swiss.

[78] The Battle of the Atlantic raged the whole War long. HMS Hood was the world's largest warship. In the Battle of Denmark Strait, fought on May 24th, HMS Hood and HMS Prince of Wales fought the German warships Bismarck and Prinz Eugen, which were trying to break out into the North Atlantic to destroy Allied merchant shipping. Less than 10 minutes after the British opened fire, a shell from Bismarck struck Hood, which sank within a few minutes. The Prince of Wales suffered serious malfunctions in her main armament, and soon broke off the engagement. The Bismarck had to abort her Atlantic mission due to damage. The Royal Navy gave chase and, two days later, while heading for occupied France, Bismarck was attacked by torpedo bombers from the aircraft carrier HMS Ark Royal. The next morning, May 27th, Bismarck was crippled by the British fleet's sustained bombardment, and was scuttled by her crew.

But in return we have sunk the Bismarck, one of their biggest ships. Mum went south and she is going to spend the nights in a shelter in London.

Lady Guise, Philippa's Mum, at Househill, Nairn, in her Red Cross uniform. Both Lady Guise and Sir Anselm, who joined the Home Guard, were keen to "do their bit" for the War effort.

4

The War Diary: aged 15

June 10th

I am 15. I had my presents after lunch. Got from Mum and Dad a gramophone and half-a-dozen records, a riding stick from Gran and from Aunt Lulla,[79] stamps from Mrs Cook and a purse from Jamie. Had a lovely big cake. We have a land-girl in the garden. Went to dancing class with Mrs Grant in the Station Hotel, Inverness.[80]

June 18th

Aunt Bunny came to stay. She had brought two oranges, which we portioned out. I have not seen oranges for ages. In the evening we took the four ponies and rode over to Lochloy.[81]

June 22nd

Germany has invaded Russia.[82] Everyone thinks Hitler must be mad. It shows he must need the wheat and oil from the Ukraine. We do hope he has bitten off more than he

---

[79] A sister of Grampapa, Sir James Augustus Grant.
[80] Philippa attended dancing classes with Mrs Grant, most often at the Highland Hotel in Nairn.
[81] Lochloy House is 3½ miles from Nairn.
[82] Germany invaded Russia at 4am GMT on this day.

can chew. His excuse was to protect Europe from the scavenging wild beast, Russia.

June 24th

The Russians are not doing too badly. The Germans are making a pincer movement towards Kiev, it is thought.

The girls and their ponies at Househill: from left to right, Philippa on Ebony, Ursula on Clover, Deb the dog, Anne Murray on Pepper and Mary Grant on Salt.

June 25th

Went to tea at Kilravock.[83] The girls are nice. Hugh is a charming boy. Rather ugly, but a nice face and good manners. After

[83] Kilravock Castle in Inverness-shire is the seat of the Rose family, heads of the clan Rose. Philippa became particular friends with Hugh Rose who was about her own age. His sisters were Elizabeth and Maddie.

tea played tennis and then went round the castle.

July 2nd

The Russians seem to be putting up a good fight, but are getting slowly driven back. They must beat the Germans. The health of the British Isles is said to be better in wartime than peace because of the lack of meat.

August 26th

We British have invaded Persia.[84] Russians still holding out.

August 27th

Spent the day grouse-driving. There were six guns and some 30 beaters. Us three and two others were flankers. They shot about 63 brace with four drives. It rained all day and we got very wet. We had a good lunch. Tom, the blacksmith, who was also a beater, found me some white heather.[85]

---

[84] Soviet, British and other Commonwealth armed forces invaded the Imperial State of Iran on August 25th, the action lasting until September 17th, 1941. The Allies' sought to secure Iranian oil fields and supply lines for the USSR's campaign against Axis forces on the Eastern Front. The Anglo-Soviet victors forced the abdication of the pro-Axis Shah on September 16th, in favour of his son Mohammad Reza Pahlavi (in turn overthrown by Ayatollah Ruhollah Mostafavi Musavi Khomeini in 1979).

[85] In 1884 Queen Victoria had written of her Scottish servant Mr Brown, that he: "espied a piece of white heather, and jumped off to pick it. No Highlander would

November 7th
John has passed into Winchester taking the top place.

Brother John
at Winchester College.

November 27th
We are advancing again in Libya and joined with Tobruk again, which has been isolated these months. It has stood out wonderfully well. There is still hard fighting going on all round Moscow. There are tremendous tank battles.

---

pass by it without picking it, for it was considered to bring good luck."

December 6th

Walking down the side of the road when a soldier caught hold of me and tried to pull me into his lorry. I struggled. He thought someone was coming and he let me go. It was a horrible moment. Had lunch at the Regal and we went to see *The Private Lives of Elizabeth and Essex*. Loved Errol Flynn. It was in Technicolor.

December 11th

Japan declared war on America and so has Germany. So now the whole world is at war. Japan has attacked the Philippines and Malaya etc and has sunk the Prince of Wales and another huge ship, awful.[86]

December 27th

In the evening kept up this diary and heard Mr Churchill speaking from Washington, USA, in the Senate.[87] Yesterday Hong

---

[86] The Empire of Japan declared war on the British Empire and the United States on December 7th, 1941 (December 8th in Japan), after Japan had attacked America's Pacific fleet at Pearl Harbor, Hawaii, that same morning. There were simultaneous Japanese attacks on the US-held Philippines and on the British Empire in Malaya, Singapore, and Hong Kong. On December 10th British warships the Prince of Wales and Repulse were sunk off the east coast of Malaya. On December 11th Germany and Italy also declared war on the USA. America was now fighting on the Allied side.

[87] Three weeks after the Pearl Harbor attack, and to cheering and applause upon Capitol Hill, Churchill addressed both Houses of Congress on this day. Within

Kong fell to the Japanese.[88] In the afternoon John and Daddy went snipe-shooting at the Druim.

December 30th

Ronald and Alan Leslie-Melville came down for the day.[89] Ronald and I played golf. We are both equally bad.

December 31st

End of another year. A hard-working one for Britain and tightening of belts. All through the Battle of the Atlantic has raged. With the victory over the Bismarck for us. At the beginning of the year we had won amazing victories in Libya and reached Benghazi, but were driven back by the Germans to the Egyptian frontier leaving the isolated garrison at Tobruk. Now under Auchinleck[90]

---

his longer speech, Philippa heard Churchill tell how the inter-war sundering of the Anglo-American special relationship had opened the way for others' war-mongering that had now reunited the two countries.

[88] The Battle of Hong Kong (East Asian dates, December 8th to 25th) was one of the first battles of the Pacific Campaign. On the same morning as the attack on Pearl Harbor, Japanese forces had invaded British Hong Kong and met stiff resistance from local troops as well as British, Canadian and Indian units. In less than a week the defenders abandoned the mainland and, less than two weeks later, unable to hold the island, the colony surrendered.

[89] See footnote to April 29th, 1941.

[90] Field Marshal Sir Claude John Eyre Auchinleck. In July 1941 he had been appointed Commander-in-Chief of the Middle East theatre but, after initial successes, the North

we have once again reached Benghazi and seem to be doing well. We have also taken Abyssinia and restored Haile Selassie.[91] Greece and Yugoslavia fell to Germany and Hungary, Bulgaria and Rumania went over to the Axis. In June, Germany invaded Russia and advanced fairly rapidly despite heavy losses. Much guerrilla fighting. Hitler failed to take Leningrad and Sebastopol. Now he has come within 40 miles of Moscow, when suddenly he found himself hurled back by the Russians, who have completely taken the initiative. The Japs attacked the Philippines and many other Pacific Islands, while still carrying on conversations with the US, who now at last have declared war on the Axis. Churchill is in the US. Hong Kong has fallen.

1942

January 4th

Finished *Beau Geste*, I enjoyed every word.

January 8th

Got dressed for the ball, then went to be viewed by Gran and Daddy. Arrived at the

---

African Campaign turned against the British and he was to be relieved of the post in 1942 during the crucial Alamein campaign.

[91] See footnote to April 6th, 1941.

Royal Hotel at 9.45, we had the Seaforth band. Everyone danced their feet off. I danced with Sandy Leslie-Melville and Ronald L-M,[92] Robert Pierson, Duncan Davidson,[93] Hugh Rose,[94] the officers and brother John. I wore my long white dress and Ursula a blue and purple dress. She looked very pretty. I thoroughly enjoyed myself, dancing every dance. An officer ran after Ursula all the evening, telling her she has lovely brown eyes. She is two years older than me and is now 17.

January 24th

Very bad news at the moment. Singapore in imminent danger. Reverses in Libya. But Russia is slowly pushing back the Germans.

January 27th

Did lessons in the afternoon, because we went to see *The Four Feathers* in the evening. Played ice hockey. Snow blocking the roads and Canadian snow plough is lost somewhere in the snow. Went to guides. Terrific wind. My skylight flew off.

---

[92] See footnote to April 29th, 1941.

[93] In fact, 16-year-old Duncan Davidson Boulton, the son of Sir Denis Boulton, 3rd Bt. Having gained the rank of Lieutenant in the Grenadier Guards, Duncan was to lose his life in February 1944 at Monte Cassino in Operation Avenger, the second of the four main attacks. See footnote to May 18th, 1944.

[94] See footnote to June 25th, 1941.

1942 **January 30th**

Bad news. Malaya has been taken and we are now defending Singapore Island itself, besides the Philippines and Dutch East Indies etc. Also danger to Australia. Now Rommel has taken the offensive in Libya, retaken Benghazi. Russia still doing well.

February 14th

Singapore has fallen. What a tragedy. The Japs have taken 60,000 prisoners. Malaya has gone, Burma crumbling.

February 16th

Jamie has got measles at school. Granny has immediately sent him her oranges and some chocolate. The Scharnhorst and Prinz Eugen have escaped from Brest up the Channel into the North Sea.[95]

¤

By November 1941 the Allies had succeeded in dislodging the Italians from East Africa. Ranked against the Italians had been the forces of Britain and Belgium and their colonies, South Africa, Free Ethiopia and Free France. In Britain the East

---

[95] At 11pm on 11th February, the three warships Scharnhorst, Gneisenau, and Prinz Eugen had sailed from their dry dock at Brest in Brittany on a "Channel Dash" to Wilhelmshaven on Germany's North Sea shore. The ships were attacked, and *Scharnhorst* hit, by British warplanes, but all three did escape.

African Campaign victories gave rise to a mock radio broadcast at the Italians' expense. It circulated in written form and depended upon the name of the laxative Cascara, which sounded like an East African town. One copy of this joke fell into my hands, and I sent it on to my brother John at Winchester. Nowadays the toilet humour needs priming with further information: Alvar Liddel often read the news on the radio; and "Jerries", a slang word for Germans, were also chamber pots.

Broadcast: This is the Home and Forces Programme. Here is the news, and this is Alvar Liddell reading it. It was learned from British United Press early this morning that a large number of Italians had taken Cascara on the border of Sudan and are now hastening to the banks of the Nile. British GHQ, while admitting that Cascara has been taken, expresses doubt as to the ability of the Italians to hold it. This seems to be confirmed by the latest reports that the Italians are evacuating all along the line, and the strain on their rear must be tremendous. The Italians tried to suppress it but it leaked out in several places. There is strong evidence that a wholesome respect is growing for the historic scrap of paper. Additional information just received states that 1,000 Jerries are being rushed to the Italians and that mopping-up operations are in progress. That is the end of the news and, as we have two minutes in hand before the next part of the programme, I will play you some chamber music.

The "historic scrap of paper" is, of course, a toilet roll. I thought all this was so funny that I was determined my brother John should not lose it. I wrote to him:

You dare lose this copy! I haven't got time to write out another for you. So could you please bring this one back with you at Easter. Don't forget please. PG.

¤

February 20th

Ann Fitzpatrick's father is missing. There are casualties from Singapore and Libya, where we are retreating.

February 26th

The Japs are advancing in Burma and Java. The Russians are still doing well. Quiet in Libya.

March 19th

Rationing becoming more severe. No more petrol for civilians after July. Coupons for clothes and no more white bread. Our ships must be saved.

March 29th

The King spoke at 9pm. Very good. Chief point was a National day of Prayer. He stammered badly.[96]

---

[96] George VI wrestled with a crippling stammer throughout his life.

March 30th

We have made a combined raid on St. Nazaire,[97] German submarines have been too successful.

April 2nd

Granny very ill, she has a bad heart. The Japs are slowly pushing us back in Burma. Sir Stafford Cripps is in India trying to come to some arrangement about self-government for them. General MacArthur of the Philippines has gone to Australia. Russia still pushing back the Germans.

April 7th

John and me went to the cinema and saw Anna Neagle in a good film.[98] In the news reel we saw a scene from the fighting in Burma.

April 10th

India has rejected our offer of self-government made by Sir Stafford Cripps.[99]

---

[97] On March 28th the Royal Navy and British commandos under Combined Operations Headquarters staged an amphibious raid and destroyed the heavily defended dry dock at St Nazaire in German-occupied France. Only 228 of the 622 British fighters came back home, as 169 died and 215 taken prisoner. See footnote to April 17th, 1942.

[98] This might have been Anna Neagle's 1941 movie *Sunny*.

[99] In the wartime coalition Government, Labour politician Cripps petitioned Indian nationalist leaders to rally their religious constituencies in support of the British Empire, on the understanding that an Allied victory would lead to Indian independence. Neither Mohandas Karamchand

Japan has sunk two of our cruisers and an aircraft carrier.[100] Very bad news.

London and Wiltshire.

April 17th

Very excited to be going south, but disappointed to be missing a dance at Darnaway.[101] Caught the sleeper train. Arrived Euston 10am. The first time I have been in London since the air raids. There are open patches of rubble, but London is full and busy. The Congreves took Marygold and me to a Beethoven concert in the evening at the Cambridge Theatre.[102] Marygold is looking very smart. Sir Adrian Boult conducted and Moiseiwitsch played the piano.[103]

Gandhi for the Hindus, nor Muhammad Ali Jinnah for the Muslims, would back the Allies against the Nazis.

[100] The Japanese Navy's prolonged Indian Ocean Raid of March 31st to April 10th struck Allied shipping and sea bases, destroying one aircraft carrier, two cruisers, two destroyers, three other naval craft, 23 merchant ships and more than 40 aircraft. Japan lost fewer than 30 aircraft.

[101] Darnaway Castle near Forres in Morayshire is the seat of the Earls of Moray.

[102] Marygold was the daughter of old family friends Lt Commander Sir Geoffrey Congreve, 1st Bt, RN, and Lady Congreve, of Turleigh Mill, Bath. Aged 44, Sir Geoffrey had been among the 169 British servicemen killed 18 days earlier at St Nazaire (see footnote to March 30th, 1942).

[103] Sir Adrian Boult had founded and was chief conductor of the BBC Symphony Orchestra. Benno Moiseiwitsch was a Ukranian-born British pianist.

April 26th

Went down to Turleigh Mill, Bath. The English countryside so green compared with Scotland. I had my first Walls ice cream since the war. Last night the whole house was shaken by the air raid on Bath. There is no war manufacture in Bath. It is a reprisal raid for ours on Lübeck and Rostock, where there are 500 homeless and 2,500 civilians killed.[104]

Gloucestershire.

April 27th

Went to stay at Kingscote.[105] It was lovely to see Granny Guise and Aunt Di. David has grown a lot. In the afternoon David took me on the back of his motorbike to Tetbury.

May 1st

In the afternoon Aunt Di, Gran and I went over to Elmore in a hired car as there is no civilian petrol. I love the house and garden. Aunt Di and I went round everything. Then we had tea with the villagers at their Mothers Union meeting. Saw Mr Prince the

---

104 The R.A.F. had bombed Lübeck on the night of March 28th, with Rostock being hit soon after. These air raids let to the so-called "Baedeker Blitz" retaliatory raids by the Luftwaffe on the English tourist cities of Exeter, Bath (April 25th and 26th), Norwich, York and Canterbury.

105 Philippa's Aunt Di Beaman lived with her family, including son David, at Kingscote House some 15 miles south of Elmore.

vicar.[106] He's a funny old boy always wearing long black robes when he walks round the village.

May 5th
Went to stay with Aunt Bunny, she works in a war factory.

5

The War Diary: aged 16

Househill, Nairn.

June 10th
I am 16. Sadly Granny is very ill.

July 15th
Russia is having a terrible time. The Germans are trying to cross the Don. Mummy invited young Lovat Scouts officers up for a drink.[107] They are to come and ride with us.

---

[106] Rev Percy E. Prince was vicar of Elmore from 1914 to 1945, seeing the village through both World Wars.
[107] The Lovat Scouts were a British Army unit first formed in January 1900 during the Second Boer War as a Scottish Highland yeomanry regiment. They were the brainchild of Simon Joseph Fraser, 14th Lord Lovat, uncle of David Stirling (creator of the Special Air Service), and of his brother Hugh, whose letter to Lovat Scout Sandy Fraser can be read in section 10 of this book. In July 1942 the

August 9th
Granny Grant died today, Sunday at 11.20am. It really is the best thing, as she was so ill, she could never have got better, but it is awful to think she will not be with us anymore. She died very peacefully. Mum was there. I cried.

August 10th
Mr Gandhi has been arrested with the rest of the Congress Party. Riots in Bombay.[108] The Russians are still falling back in the Caucasus.

August 16th
Mr Churchill flew to Moscow.

September 1st
Mary and I went to see *Pygmalion* with Leslie Howard and Wendy Hiller.[109] Mary expects her father back from Egypt. They have not seen him for four years.

Scouts were newly back from the Faroe Islands, where they had been ready for a German invasion. In December 1943 they would be sent to Canada for ski and mountain training, joining the Italian Campaign from mid-1944.

[108] On August 8th at the All-India Congress Committee session in Bombay, Gandhi launched the anti-British "Quit India" movement. The next day, Gandhi, Nehru and many other leaders of the Indian National Congress were arrested by the British Government. Over the next several days disorderly and non-violent demonstrations took place throughout India.

[109] The 1938 film of George Bernard Shaw's stage play.

September 3rd

War was declared 3 years ago. A National day of Prayer. Went to church in Auldearn as Dad was on parade there.[110]

September 19th

Leningrad still holding out. Read *The Snow Goose: A Story of Dunkirk.*[111] Played with Jamie as usual.

Scone Palace, Perthshire.

September 23rd

No more governesses for me. I was sent to my first school aged 16, at Scone Palace where the kings of Scotland were crowned. The school had been evacuated from Edinburgh. Mum took me to Craigmount School evacuated to Scone Palace. Miss Ross the headmistress met us, she seems to have quite a sense of humour. I sleep in a dormitory.

October 7th

We hear the news with Miss Ross every evening. Stalingrad is still holding out. Wonderful. A heap of ruins and dead. News is a little better.

---

[110] Auldern is a village a short way outside Nairn.

[111] *The Snow Goose: A Story of Dunkirk* by the American writer Paul Gallico was first published in 1940 as a short story. Gallico had then expanded it as a novella, first published on April 7th, 1941.

October 28th

Stalingrad still holding out. Miraculous. General Smuts in England.[112] New offensive in Egypt.[113] Successful naval battle in the Pacific.[114]

October 31st

Went to see *The First of the Few* with David Niven and Leslie Howard about the creation of the Spitfire. V.G.

November 4th

Just heard that Hugh Rose has been killed in Egypt.[115] So sad. Such a nice boy. It is such a shock, when someone of one's own age dies. So sorry for Mrs Rose and Elizabeth and

---

[112] Jan Smuts' second term as Prime Minister of South Africa was from 1939 to 1948. He had been the most senior South African to argue against declaring neutrality towards Germany. In 1941 Smuts had been appointed a field marshal of the British Army. He had arrived in England on October 14th for talks with the Government.

[113] El Alamein in northern Egypt had witnessed an inconclusive battle in July 1942. But between October 23rd and November 4th, Allied forces broke the Axis line and forced them all the way back to Tunisia. This ended German and Italian hopes of occupying Egypt, seizing the Suez Canal and gaining access to the Middle Eastern oil fields. Drawing Axis fire into this second front also gave some relief to the USSR on the Eastern Front.

[114] The Battle of Santa Cruz Islands was fought October 25th to 27th. Japanese naval forces engaged the US Navy in support of an amphibious offensive against Allied possession of Guadalcanal and other nearby islands. In the fighting, the US lost a carrier, but inflicted severe aircrew losses on the Japanese.

[115] See footnotes to June 25th, 1941, and October 28th, 1942.

Maddie. Ice on the curling pond. The Brahan Seer said that when the gooseberry bush in the tower at Kilravock died, the last Rose would die also.[116] The gooseberry died at the beginning of the war. And we all knew. The parents were all talking about it.

November 5th

We have had the most glorious victory over the Italians and Germans in Egypt.[117] They are retreating fast and about time too.

November 9th

Went to see Charlie Chaplin in *The Gold Rush*.

November 10th

The Americans have taken Algiers and Morocco. Rommel is still fleeing before us. Heard Churchill speak on wireless.[118] Very amusing and encouraging.

---

[116] Named for Brahan Castle near Dingwall in Ross-shire, the seat of clan MacKenzie, this seer known as Coinneach Odhar, or Kenneth Mackenzie, was either a Victorian folklorist's invention, or a real character of the 1600s. Several events are said to have been foretold by him, although none of the foretellings exist in his autograph, and most of the manuscripts post-date the events themselves.

[117] On November 4th at 5.30pm the Axis forces at El Alamein began to retreat. It was the beginning of the end of the North Africa Campaign.

[118] Churchill's speech at the Lord Mayor of London's Mansion House luncheon, known as The End of the Beginning, included these words about Allied advances in

November 11th

Armistice Day. Sad to be in the middle of another terrible war.

November 12th

Germany has now marched into all unoccupied France. The French Toulon fleet, thank goodness, resists them.[119] It is a very critical moment for us in N. Africa. Especially a race for Tunis.[120]

North Africa: "Now this is not the end. It is not even the beginning of the end. But it is, perhaps, the end of the beginning . . . We mean to hold our own. I have not become the King's First Minister in order to preside over the liquidation of the British Empire. For that task, if ever it were prescribed, someone else would have to be found, and, under democracy, I suppose the nation would have to be consulted. I am proud to be a member of that vast commonwealth and society of nations and communities gathered in and around the ancient British monarchy, without which the good cause might well have perished from the face of the earth. Here we are, and here we stand, a veritable rock of salvation in this drifting world."

[119] Having lost control of North Africa, Germany on November 11th seized France's Mediterranean shores by occupying Corsica and invading Vichy France. Of high value was the Vichy fleet of three battleships, seven cruisers, 28 destroyers and 20 submarines in the Mediterranean harbour of Toulon. Vichy forces did not fight the German invasion but French naval commanders did delay the handover of vessels for long enough to plan and execute the scuttling of the fleet at Toulon on November 27th.

[120] Tunis, the capital of Tunisia, was held by Axis forces from November 1942 to May 1943. After being hemmed about by Allied forces from Algeria in the west and Libya in the east, it became the last Axis base in Africa, from which they would flee to Italy.

November 15th

The church bells rang this morning for the first time to celebrate our victory in Egypt. But normally the bells are to be rung to tell us we have been invaded.

November 16th

A good talk after the news on landings in Algiers.[121] The Americans have had a great victory over the Japs in the Solomon Islands. 23 boats sunk.[122]

November 21st

In the afternoon went to the theatre in Perth and saw *Hedda Gabler* by Ibsen. V.G.

November 24th

The Russians have advanced and encircled the German Army round Stalingrad, 50,000 prisoners taken. Wonderful after all these months of siege. The whole of French W.

---

[121] Operation Torch from November 8th to 11th was the Anglo-American invasion of Vichy French Morocco and Algeria. During Operation Torch, leading Vichy politician and Admiral François Darlan happened to be in Algiers. As part of a swiftly done deal with the Allies, on November 10th Darlan had called on all French forces to join the invasion against the Axis powers. On December 24th Darlan was assassinated by an anti-Nazi French-Algerian.

[122] The Naval Battle of Guadalcanal in the Solomon Islands from November 12th to 15th saw the Japanese decisively repulsed from their efforts to dislodge the Americans. The Japanese lost 15 boats, not 23.

Africa has become our ally. What a lovely change to have good news.

November 30th

I have got my hair turned under as a page boy. Mr Churchill spoke last night. Not quite so good as usual as he had only good news!

December 6th

Went to church. I hate walking in a crocodile. Smoked a cigarette in the dormitory last night.

December 31st

Well, this is the end of 1942, a year of war and much sorrow. It started with a dark outlook and has ended with a much brighter one. Last Christmas Hong Kong had fallen and the Japs were overrunning the Pacific, nearly capturing India and Australia. After the catastrophe of Singapore we were indeed depressed. However, the Americans recaptured part of the Solomon Islands and after a stubborn fight we have been victorious in Burma and New Guinea. At the beginning of the year we had advanced as far as Benghazi, in North Africa. However, we soon had to retreat right back into Egypt and this time losing Tobruk. Germans within 60 miles of Alexandria. A very bad state of affairs. However, now under Montgomery we have dealt Rommel a crushing blow and advanced far beyond Benghazi and we are now on the way to Tunis.[123] The Americans and us have landed a huge force in Algiers, but have not yet captured the port of Bizerta.[124] The whole of French North Africa came over to the allies under Darlan who has now been assassinated. Germany has taken Vichy France and the French Toulon fleet sunk itself, thereby recovering the glory of France. Stalingrad, covered in snow and millions dead.

1943

January 20th

Excellent news all round except perhaps in Tunisia. Russians advancing. Relieved the siege of Leningrad. Advanced and taken Mazrata in Libya.[125] Taken Samolan in New Guinea.[126]

---

[123] Philippa's first naming of the North Africa Campaign's two opposing Field Marshals: Bernard Law Montgomery, commander of the Eighth Army, from August 1942 in the Western Desert until the final Allied victory in Tunisia; and of Erwin Johannes Eugen Rommel, commander of joint German and Italian forces.

[124] Bizerta or Bizerte in Tunisia was occupied by the German Army and would not be taken by American troops until May 7th, 1943.

[125] Mazra`at Katarilla, about 60 miles southeast of Tripoli.

[126] Salamaua was a small administrative town and port on a small isthmus on Papua New Guinea's northeast shore. The closest city is Lae, 22 miles to the north, which can only be reached by boat across the gulf. By 1942 the

January 23rd

Went to see *Mrs Miniver* with Greer Garson and Walter Pidgeon.

January 25th

The Union Jack now flies over Tripoli and Rommel is still fleeing before us.

February 8th

Churchill back in England after having been in Casablanca (the Unconditional peace meeting).[127]

Japanese had established major bases in Lae and in Salamaua, the latter as a staging post for attacks on Port Moresby on New Guinea's southeast shore. When the attacks failed, the Japanese turned Salamaua into a major supply base. In the January 29th to 31st, 1943, Battle of Wau the Japanese would attack Wau, an Australian base about 25 miles away, which potentially threatened the Japanese positions at Salamaua and Lae. The Japanese were repulsed.

[127] The Casablanca Conference was held at the Anfa Hotel in Casablanca in the French protectorate of Morocco, from January 14th to 24th, 1943, to plan the Allied European strategy for the next phase of the War. In attendance were US President Franklin D. Roosevelt, British Prime Minister Winston Churchill, and Generals Charles de Gaulle and Henri Giraud representing the Free French forces. USSR premier Joseph Stalin did not attend, citing the Stalingrad conflict as requiring him to stay in the Soviet Union. The Conference issued the demand for "unconditional surrender" of all Axis members.

1943 **February 12th**

Had dancing in the evening. I did the quickstep and foxtrot with Pip and tango and waltz with Andrea.[128]

February 15th

The Russians have taken Rostov and so have surrounded the German Caucasian army.

May 7th

The 1st Army has taken Tunis and Bizerta. Quicker than anyone thought. I suppose Mike Beaman[129] is there. Already 20,000 prisoners of war. The 8th Army from Egypt, the Americans and the French are there also.

May 13th

All resistance has now ceased in Tunisia. Dunkirk is at last avenged. A great victory, but unfortunately many casualties.

May 14th

In the evening Churchill spoke from Washington about the Home Guard. The campaign from El Alamein to Tunisia is now completely finished. The Mediterranean is open to our shipping. We have taken 170,000 prisoners including some generals.

---

[128] Pip and Andrea were friends at the dancing class.

[129] Mike Beaman was Philippa's first cousin, six years older than her, and in the Army.

May 16th

Our bombers bombed three of the Ruhr great dams and have in consequence flooded many towns and works of the Ruhr.

May 19th

Mr Churchill spoke to the US Congress. Full of good humour. V.G.

May 25th

The biggest raid of the war on Sicily and S. Italy. All quiet in N. Africa. Russia is in a deadlock. Churchill still in USA.

May 27th

The Russians have given up their international Comintern.[130] Now no fear of socialism, so an even firmer alliance.

June 7th

Pantelleria and Lampadusa, two Italian islands,[131] surrendered to us on account of bombing. Good.

---

[130] The USSR's Communist International had been set up on March 2nd, 1919, to fight "by all available means, including armed force, for the overthrow of the international bourgeoisie and for the creation of an international Soviet republic as a transition stage to the complete abolition of the State." It was itself abolished on May 15th, 1943.

[131] These Mediterranean islands are closer to Libya than to Italy.

6

The War Diary: aged 17

June 21st
The King is in North Africa.

June 25th
The King has had a wonderful reception in Malta. Our raids on Germany are growing heavier and heavier.

July 10th
The invasion of Sicily has begun. I wonder if Mike is there?

August 14th
The war news is nearly all good. Catania and Randazzo both captured and Germans evacuating Sicily.[132] Rome declared an open city.[133] Milan in confusion. Hamburg and many other German towns flat. Russians great advances in the Urals,[134] Krakow[135] and Smolensk.[136] Churchill again in USA. Pacific quiet.

---

[132] Catania and Randazzo are in the east of Sicily.
[133] Meaning the Italian authorities have opened Rome to Allied occupation.
[134] The Urals run as a ridge from the Kara Sea in the north to the Aral Sea in the south (which was then the USSR's Kazakh Soviet Socialist Republic).
[135] In Poland.
[136] In Russia.

September 8th

A great day of victories. Italy has surrendered unconditionally. The Russians have recaptured the Donets Basin.[137]

Edinburgh.

September 20th

Went to The Edinburgh College of Art, Lauriston Place. Andrea and I have digs out at Morningside. We come rattling down over cobbled streets each morning in a tram for a penny 3 farthings. Penny Beaton teaches me.[138] I am a fresher. Mrs Macdonald is our landlady. She gives us for breakfast scrambled eggs and they are made out of dried powdered egg, but quite good.

September 28th

Went to the Royal Ballet and sat up in the gods as we were students. Looked down on the whole stage and watched Margot Fonteyn dancing beautifully in Swan Lake and Robert Helpmann being an amazing mimic in another ballet [139]

---

[137] The east of the Ukrainian Soviet Socialist Republic.

[138] Penelope Beaton was an artist and teacher who, in the 1930s, had been particularly influenced by Sir William Gillies.

[139] English ballerina Margot Fonteyn and Australian dancer Robert Helpmann who, in 1942, produced three of his own ballets, *Comus*, *Hamlet* and *The Birds*. For the Royal Ballet in 1942 the two starred together in his *Hamlet*.

October 3rd

Dick Allhusen took us round war memorials.[140] He is in the Lovat Scouts.

November 16th

Russians still victorious. Have won back the River Dnieper.[141] 8th and 5th Armies advancing up Italy (the Allies). Trouble with the French Lebanon.[142]

November 23rd

The heaviest raid of the war on Berlin. 2,300 tons of bombs! Russians' grim struggle round Kiev. Bad weather stops operations in

---

[140] Richard Christian "Dick" Allhusen, aged 33, son of Frederick Allhusen of Fulmer House, Buckinghamshire, was a first cousin of Madeline, Lady Congreve, born Allhusen (see footnote to April 17th, 1942). In 1908 Dick's father had been recruited as a major to the Lovat Scouts.

[141] The Dnieper rises in the Valdai Hills between Petersburg and Moscow, flowing through Russia, Belarus and Ukraine to the Black Sea. The Red Army's Lower Dnieper Offensive, to take back the east bank from the Germans, had several operational phases from August 24th to December 23rd, 1943.

[142] France had the League of Nations Mandate to rule the Lebanese after World War One. In 1941 the Mandate had passed from Vichy to Free French governance, and on November 26th Lebanese national independence had been declared albeit within the framework of the French Mandate. On November 8th, 1943, a newly elected Lebanese Government dissolved the Mandate. The Free French authorities promptly gaoled the President and his Government. This "trouble" identified by Philippa led to an armed resistance, the nascent Lebanese Army. On November 22nd, 1943, the Free French at last freed the Government and recognised its sovereignty in Lebanon.

Italy. Lebanon still in rebellion against the French. We have lost the islands of Samos and Leros.

December 1st

My friend at Edinburgh College of Art, Mary Thompson, has just had her call-up papers aged 18 and 6 months. I feel sorry for her and a bit shaken myself.

December 2nd

Mr Churchill is in Cairo with Chiang Kai-shek and Roosevelt for conference on Japan.[143]

December 5th

Meeting of Churchill, Stalin and Roosevelt in Iran reached complete agreement.[144]

---

[143] The Cairo Conference in Egypt, from 22nd to 26th November, ended with Britain's Churchill, America's Roosevelt, and leader of the Chinese nationalist militarist Republic, Chiang Kai-shek, declaring that Imperial Japan must surrender unconditionally to the Allies, restoring to their previous sovereignties all territories won during the War, and to China all territories that seemed ever to have been "stolen". The USSR's Stalin stayed away due to the Soviet-Japanese Neutrality Pact that affirmed Russia was not at war with Japan, although allied to Japan's enemies. Meeting with Chiang may have provoked Japan, so Stalin met with Churchill and Roosevelt from November 28th to December 1st at the Teheran Conference in Iran.

[144] The Teheran Conference agreed to support the Yugoslav Partisans, to urge Turkey out of neutrality as one of the Allies, and to invade France from Britain.

December 29th

We have sunk the Scharnhorst and three German destroyers in the Bay of Biscay.[145] Good.

December 31st

Went to have a look at all the landing barges, etc. This area is now combined ops. The three of us stayed up for the first time to see the New Year in and sang *Auld Lang Syne.*

1944

Gloucestershire.

March 2nd

In the morning Mike and I again rode.[146] We are very good friends. I am very fond of him.

---

[145] The Battle of North Cape on December 26th saw the German battlecruiser Scharnhorst brought to battle from its mission to sink the Western Allies' Arctic convoys of supplies for the Soviet Union. With its greater firepower on the day, the Royal Navy sank the Scharnhorst off Norway's North Cape. On December 27th, as part of the Allies' Operation Stonewall to blockade German imports along the French coast, the R.A.F. sank the armed supply ship Alsterufer; but not before 11 German warships had sailed into the Bay of Biscay to meet and escort her. This flotilla turned back to its base but on the 28th and in bad weather it was intercepted by two Royal Navy ships, HMS Glasgow and HMS Enterprise, which sank three of the 11 German vessels and damaged a further four.

[146] Philippa had left Househill for a short stay with Mike Beaman's parents at Kingscote House.

At any rate he doesn't seem to mind my company. We chatted about girls, death on the front line, etc. I think he takes me as a sister. He has got 300 miles of leave-petrol and so we drove over to Elmore. I drove in the lanes. He is very interesting about Italy, etc. Elmore just lovely, but this time it doesn't seem to be so big! We visited the churchyard and went to see the Coldricks and the Finches.[147] I long to be back there. On the way back Mike and I chatted about being grown-up, a sense of humour and character. Felt awfully sad at the thought of leaving.

Edinburgh.

May 18th

Cassino has at last fallen to us and we seem to be on the move in Italy after a three months' pause.[148]

---

[147] Mr Coldrick, Elmore Court's groom and chauffeur, had also taught Philippa to ride. Mrs Finch had been Granny Guise's lady's maid before the War.

[148] The Battle of Monte Cassino from January 17th to May 18th, 1944, comprised four main Allied assaults against German and Italian troops on the defensive Winter Line that ran from Italy's west to east coasts. Central to the fighting were the ruins of Cassino's ancient Abbey. The Winter Line had to be breached before Rome could be taken, which it was after great loss of Allied lives.

1944 **June 6th**

D-Day! The invasion day. We have landed a colossal invasion in France at Caen.[149] The real day has come. Oh! Who will be killed? I only hope Mike and Alan are through safely.[150] A terrific sense of relief.

June 7th

Invasion still going on. We have secured the beach heads in Normandy.

7

The War Diary: aged 18

June 11th

Did my diary survey of being 17 and then discovered I had no less than 18 urgent letters to write. So wrote and then conked out.

---

[149] June 6th, D-Day, saw the opening action of Operation Overlord, the Battle of Normandy. Shortly after midnight 24,000 British, American and Canadian airborne troops landed inland in Normandy. From 6.30am more than 160,000 troops were landed amphibiously on to Normandy's beaches to secure beachheads for further landing of equipment and supplies. The Allies had meant to take Caen, one of Normandy's largest cities, for its strategic value on D-Day. In fact the Battle for Caen went on until the Germans were finally beaten on August 6th.

[150] Mike Beaman was in the King's Royal Rifles Corps. Royal Navy sailor Alan Ross was the nephew of Miss Ross, headmistress at Craigmount School, Scone Palace.

June 16th

The invasion still going well. We have a 60-mile beachhead now. Both the King and Churchill in France. Pushing ahead in Italy. Germans started robot raids (doodlebugs).

June 22nd

Thank goodness I have passed the College of Art first-year exams. Went to metalwork.

July 20th

An attempt on Hitler's life said to be by prominent Nazi general.[151] Confusion in the Reich. The Russians are simply sweeping over Poland. Normandy slow but sure. Leghorn and Orvieto just fallen in Italy. People say the end the war is very close. I feel I can hardly bear the worry of it all.

July 21st

I am madly reading *Gone with the Wind*.

July 22nd

I am longing to get fixed for either the WRNS or the Free FANYs and go south [152]

---

[151]The July 20th assassination attempt against Adolf Hitler aimed to seize political control of Germany and her armed forces from the Nazis. Hitler survived the explosion at his Wolf's Lair field headquarters in Rastenburg, East Prussia, and consequently a planned military coup foundered as the conspirators lost nerve.

[152] The First Aid Nursing Yeomanry (FANY) was founded in 1907 to rescue and nurse injured servicemen. In September 1938 FANY was asked to form the initial Motor

and do something. Mum I think realizes it, but Dad hasn't the foggiest.

Househill, Nairn.

July 23rd

I drove Dad up to Fornighty for the Home Guard. My longest drive yet.[153]

July 30th

Ursula and I went up to the R.A.F. Brakla canteen to help.[154] Then picnicked on the beach. We bicycle everywhere.

August 8th

Everyone lives in high hopes of victory. I remain sceptical. I have learnt too well to fear the Germans. Russia has poured over Poland to the outskirts of Warsaw and East Prussia. There has been a large revolt among the German generals. We are advancing up Italy. Normandy is slow work. The

---

Driver Companies of the Auxiliary Territorial Service, called the Women's Transport Service. While most FANYs were absorbed into the ATS, there were some who did not transfer. These "Free FANYs" provided ambulances and ran mobile canteens. Also, over two thousand FANYs were seconded to the SOE, a paramilitary organisation established in July 1940 with the intention of "setting Europe ablaze."

[153] Fornighty is about seven miles southeast of Nairn.

[154] R.A.F. Brackla was near the small village of Piperhill, about four miles south of Nairn, and was a Relief Landing Ground for R.A.F. Dalcross, now Inverness Airport, about eight miles west of Brackla.

Americans have just swept all over the Brittany peninsula and are on their way to Paris. Caen is the hinge of the German defence. The casualties seem high. So dreadful. Practically all the people I know out there have been killed or wounded, except Mike, thank God. Donald Wallace,[155] my friend, and Ronnie Mackintosh-Walker from Geddes,[156] a great friend of Aunt

---

[155] A lieutenant in the Black Watch, Donald Wallace was the son of Col. Robert Wallace of that Ilk. Donald was killed aged 20 in Normandy on July 1st, 1944. Philippa includes below, among the wounded, Donald's brother Malcolm who was mentioned in despatches and in 1945 became a major in the Black Watch.

[156] Geddes is about three miles south of Househill. Margaret (Philippa's Mum) and Hester Grant (Aunt Bunny) had been childhood friends with Ronnie "Mac Wac" (as the Mackintosh-Walkers were known). Young Ronnie grew to be Brigadier Ronnie Mackintosh-Walker commanding the 227th (Highland) Infantry Brigade from July 29th, 1942, until he was killed on July 17th, 1944, aged 46. The following was written about his death by Nigel Chastel de Boinville in 2003: "My father, Charles de Boinville was a captain in the Seaforth Highlanders in 1944. He was GSO2 [General Staff Officer (Grade 2) ranked a major] of a brigade in Normandy, with Major John Lochore as Brigade Major, and Mackintosh-Walker as Brigadier. All were Seaforth Highlanders. The Brigade, as far as I remember, consisted of battalions from the Argylls, Gordons, and H.L.I. Mackintosh-Walker had won the M.C. and bar in 1918 on the western front when he was only 18. In July 1944 when Montgomery was trying to break out, a fierce battle against tough resistance took place. Lochore who had been visiting the Argylls to assess the planning of an attack, was killed leading a charge. The next night a battle known as Monty's Moonlight began, named for the shining of searchlights onto the clouds to give light at night. Brigade HQ was in a barn in the

Bunny, I think she was going to marry him,[157] both were killed. Also Oliver Ruggles-Brise missing (just awful),[158] Ian Houldsworth,[159] Chandos Blair,[160] Malcolm Wallace all wounded.

---

middle of an orchard, but far too close to the line. At the beginning of an artillery bombardment, the Brigadier [Mackintosh-Walker] said, "Charles, let's go and look at the war." My father was a little nervous about this, as German counter-fire was falling on the orchard. He tried to persuade the Brigadier to put on his tin helmet, but the reply was, "It's too damn hot." They got into a Bren Gun Carrier [Universal Carrier] parked alongside the barn. The Brigadier was in his shirt sleeves and braces. Suddenly a barrage of German pipe-shells hit the orchard, with a loud whizzing sound. One landed and burst on the roof of the barn, and the shrapnel fell onto the Bren Gun Carrier. One piece hit Ronnie Mackintosh-Walker on the bald top of his head, killing him instantly. One piece bounced off my father's helmet, wounding him in the thigh. He then managed to get back into Brigade HQ, call one of the Battalion colonels to take command, and inform Division. The general, who, I think, was Macmillan, came up, said, "What the fuck is going on? Get this bloody HQ a mile back from the line," approved the temporary command of the Lt. Col. and returned to Divisional HQ. I don't remember the location of the orchard now, but when my father visited the site in 1971 there was a plaque on the wall commemorating Brigadier Mackintosh-Walker."

[157] Hester (Aunt Bunny) and her first husband, William Darley Bridge, had been divorced in 1938, scandalously.

[158] A lieutenant in the 2nd Armoured Battalion, Grenadier Guards, Thomas Oliver Ruggles-Brise was killed aged 21 at Caen on July 18th, 1944.

[159] A 23-year-old Territorial Army major, Ian Houldsworth of Dallas Lodge, Forres, was awarded the Territorial Decoration.

[160] A Seaforth Highlander, Major Chandos Blair MC was wounded in June, 1944, repelling an SS tank and infantry attack near Le Valtru, Normandy.

August 9th
Lady Leven has heard that Sandy has been wounded in the knee.[161]

August 14th
There is now a great deal of talk about a major victory in the Normandy Pocket, during the course of this week.[162] Eisenhower has sent a message to his staff to congratulate them.

August 26th
Rumania and Bulgaria have both sued for Peace. Paris has fallen, wonderful. The Maquis are doing great work (the French underground). We are sweeping on in both north and south France. In the afternoon I went for my medical for the Free FANYs.

September 1st
Gerald Ponsonby has been wounded in Normandy. June Ponsonby, my friend is working at the War Office.[163]

---

[161] Sandy Leslie-Melville was a captain in the Coldstream Guards. See footnote to April 29th, 1941.
[162] From August 12th to 21st was fought the Battle of the Falaise Pocket, referring to the pocket of German forces around the Normandy town of Falaise, south of Caen. The Germans had been surrounded by the Allied advance. The battle ended in the destruction of most of Germany's forces west of the Seine, opening the Allies' way to Paris and the German border.
[163] Captain Hon. Gerald and Hon. June Ponsonby were the children of Hubert Ponsonby, 5th Baron de Mauley of

September 6th

Aunt Bunny is staying. She is about to go to France in a welfare job with the troops.

September 12th

Sandy Balgonie came to lunch, has recovered from his wound.[164]

September 14th

Wrote to Mike and Alan, I think these are the two boys I am most fond of.[165] So I suppose my heart is still my own up to date!

London and Chicheley, Buckinghamshire.

September 18th

The great day! I join the Free FANYs in London, went into a room with 40 or 50 other girls. Terrifying. Spent the time signing forms, etc. All of us were taken through London in Army trucks and arrived at Chicheley Hall about tea-time.[166] Head

---

Canford. On their father's death, Gerald became the 6th Baron. Gerald died in 2002 aged 81, June in 2010 aged 82.

[164] The heir apparent of the Earldom of Leven is styled Lord Balgonie. On his father's death in 1947, Sandy became 14th Earl of Leven.

[165] See footnote to June 6th, 1944.

[166] Baroque Chicheley Hall, near Chicheley in Buckinghamshire, was used by the Special Operations Executive as its Special Training School No. 46. From 1942 until 1943 it was used for training Czechoslovaks for SOE parachute missions. It was later used to train Polish

reeling with instructions. Chicheley is a lovely place. Built 1690.[167] On parade in the morning and got drilled. Busy all day.

Government Code and Cypher School, Bletchley Park, Buckinghamshire.

September 20th

We sleep in Nissen huts in the park.[168] Very nice staff. Lots of them have their animals here, horses and dogs. Everyone is tiresomely vague about our future. In the meantime we are being taught decoding at Bletchley Park. There is a whole wall of knobs and buttons to pull and press, very complicated. Splendid and very nice ladies helping us. It seems most likely we shall be sent to India.

September 22nd

Some of the girls are very nice. We went for a long march and most of us now have blisters on our feet. We have made three great aerial landings in Holland.[169]

---

agents, and then became a FANY wireless telegraphy school.

[167] Sir John Chester started building Chicheley Hall in 1719 on the site of a far older house that he had inherited in 1698. The present house was completed in 1723.

[168] Bletchley was a small town that could not sleep Bletchley Park's very many workers, who therefore slept in Nissen huts around the park.

[169] Between September 17th and 25th, Operation Market Garden was the then biggest airborne military operation

1944 **September 28th**

We were interviewed at Bletchley. Mummy has sent a telegram saying I am not to go to India. Dreadfully depressed. I have enjoyed being in the Free FANYs and hope to heavens I will soon be back again with them. Mum didn't want me to go to India because the Japs were in Burma and most likely would invade India.

¤

September 29th [170]

Sep. 29 *Dall House* [171]
Rannoch Station
Perthshire

Darling: I'm afraid you must have had a perfectly horrid day yesterday and I feel so sorry about it and for your disappointment. When I first got your letter, I couldn't make up my mind if my extreme aversion to the idea of your going to India was just I hated the thought of your being reft from me so

---

ever, into the Netherlands and Germany, to secure bridges over the Maas, the Rhine, and other canals and watercourses, to allow speedy Allied advance into Germany. Market Garden failed to secure enough bridges and was very costly in Allied lives.

[170] After the telegram of September 28th, Philippa's mother sent her this letter giving other reasons why she wished her daughter not to go to India.

[171] Dall House was designed in 1854 by architect Thomas Mackenzie. Sir Anselm loved to be at Dall, so as to go stalking.

soon for so long or if my fears for your health and well being were really justified. As you know I went and saw Mrs Hunt who I liked so much and she naturally painted a very rosy picture, but I think a fair one. I liked her so much, however I came away feeling in my bones I ought not to let you go but hating the thought that perhaps in so doing I was taking away an experience that would be wonderful for you. Then a strange coincidence happened, there was a very nice R.A.F. officer in my carriage coming North, who had just been in India, so I asked him what sort of conditions service girls lived in and what their life was like, he said he thought they might keep fit if they were extremely careful of themselves, but of course the hot weather was very trying, but that all girls were spoilt by being out there and that no girl of your age ought to be allowed to go, then strangely enough a woman in the carriage joined in and said she had been in India, had got dysentery and suffered with her tummy all her life. By this time you can readily understand I had quite made up my mind, we couldn't let you take such risks, which was perhaps just as well, as I really don't think I could have persuaded Daddy. I do so hope they have been able to find a job for you, your telephone talk was a great relief to me, however if nothing materialises you could always join the WRNS and who knows it may be for the best. I know I can't send this letter till I know what you are going to do or where you are going to be, but I thought I would put my reasons on paper the reasons for refusing to let you go to India while they were still fresh and though you may not agree, you will know that it was not just a selfish desire to have you nearer to home.

Much love darling

Your loving Mum

¤

September 29th [172]

'B' Company
2/KRRC
29.9.44 BLA

Dear Philippa

Heil to thee Free Fanny (this is what I deciphered your letter to say) whatever that may be. I gather you will be driving some vehicle or other, so let me know whereabouts you are and I will keep well off the road, but joking apart I am sure you will drive beautifully and expect you to drive a very important general and pull strings to get me demobilised quickly when the time comes. I am glad to hear all are well at Househill and

[172] A letter from Mike Beaman, to whom his cousin Philippa had written on September 14th. KRRC is King's Royal Rifle Corps. BLA is British Liberation Army. From Mike's letter, it is clear that Philippa had asked whether he knew of Gerald Ponsonby being wounded (September 1st), or that her pet dove at Househill was in good health. Mike has news of Jimmy the kestrel, who seems to have been a soldier's pet on campaign.

you sound to have been having quite a gay time. I cannot quite place Gerald Ponsonby, but believe he has 2 sisters called Lavinia and Juliet.[173]

Life here has been very hectic. We have done much travelling and fighting with very little sleep, in fact for days I have been so tired I have been unable to think at all, but about a week ago we had a few days' rest and a day in Brussels, which really was fun, though somewhat detrimental to the Bank Balance. I cannot remember when I last wrote you, in fact my memory is becoming a little weak in my old age, but we have had good and bad times. By the time of the breakthrough we had begun to loathe the sight of mined houses, empty streets, and mined crops, and then we were dashed off to take part in the battle of Falaise, which was a bit hectic, especially as I was commanding 2 different platoons owing to shortage of officers. However we did pretty well and then had two days rest and were sent off to collect some enemy who were cut off. Unfortunately some of our own side mistook us for a counter-attack, so we had a rather

---

[173] Gerald Ponsonby's sisters were June and Winifred. Lavinia and Juliet were sisters of Ashley Ponsonby, a captain in the Coldstream Guards, who had been wounded by a German sniper in February 1944, at Monte Ornito, in the last leg of the Italian Campaign. Both sets of Ponsonbys were great-grandchildren of Charles Ponsonby, 2nd Baron de Mauley of Canford.

unpleasant hour or so, but then it was only collecting prisoners, thousands of them. We got a tremendous amount of loot including several bottles of brandy and rum each. I collected quite a few German pistols and all kinds of useful things, and lots of tinned food the best of which was asparagus. The carnage was appalling, wrecked vehicles, tanks, dead Germans, horses (their infantry transport is nearly all horse drawn). Then we were rushed along to the Seine, the whole route being strewn with wrecked vehicles etc, and there we stopped for 2 very pleasant days. We were hoping for some fly-fishing in the Risle, where we saw some tremendous trout, but on we went and my memory slightly fails me. There were day and night drives, ambushes so far ahead of our own troops that the Germans refused to believe we were enemy until we got them, driving skirmishes, no sleep, over the Somme, into Belgium, on to the borders of Holland, everywhere cheering crowds and bottles of beer or wine, cascades of flowers and fruit, and us finding it hard to keep awake. At one moment I had a hand-to-hand encounter with a very large German, who luckily for me was despatched by one of my corporals with his 2nd attempt to crack his head with the butt of a rifle, the first having hit me on the leg. And then we were pulled back for 3 days' rest. The N of France was very pretty and much like parts of England with lots of woods and streams. Belgium is really one large market garden with quite a few canals, pretty flat, the odd wood, and houses everywhere. In fact it is the densest populated country I have ever seen, villages all close together and the roads between them lined with houses, every third one being a pub where one could buy schnapps. There was one afforested district we were in once, but that was only an exception. In Brussels there was one large black market. All the people admitted they had made fortunes out of the Germans and seemed to be enlarging them from us. We fed better than since the war began. Except for the few days we had at Cape Town, and it was just like a pre-war city. Then on once more and we find Holland a flat land of canals, windmills, and thickly dotted with houses. I suppose now we keep going until the war here is finished, which I hope will be soon.

I am glad your Dove is well. It must be a delightful pet and I hope to see it soon. I fear it must miss you. Jimmy the kestrel having learned to fly took to stealing people's food and I think somebody must have thrown something at him. Anyway when we had a quick move one day he refused to be caught, which was rather sad, but anyway we could not have kept him during the last few weeks, without keeping him caged the whole time.

As to home news it is good, except David has been over doing it a bit so has got to take it easy. My hound is in tremendous

1944 *form and there seem to have been quite a few people staying at Kingscote and they said they hoped Aunt Margaret would soon.* [174]

As to yourself and your rude remarks about my writing, which I consider excellent, I am certain it is good exercise for my brain to decipher your letters, so if you have time from your military duties I should love to hear how they go and how you like the life, and if you have any time for Oxford Groupists or you are now a Confucianist? [175] *I hope all your animals are well and my love to all at Househill. I hope Jamie likes Stowe.* [176] *Sorry to hear the scarcity of game.*

I must finish

love

MacBeaman [177] *Mike*

---

[174] "Aunt Margaret" is Philippa's mother.

[175] The Oxford Group was centred on Evangelical Christian symposia rather than worship. It had great influence through the 1930s in Britain and abroad, had in 1938 called not for military but "moral re-armament", and during the war (while also contributing members to the armed forces) had encouraged civilian work for the swifter defeat of the Axis. By 1939 it had been thoroughly rebranded as MRA – Moral Re-Armament. Interest in Confucianism as an alternative to communism and liberal democracy was prompted in the 1930s as Chinese leader Chiang Kai-shek developed the New Life Movement, fusing Confucian courtesy with authoritarian nationalism and Christianity.

[176] Philippa's youngest brother Jamie had been sent to Stowe School in Buckinghamshire.

[177] "MacBeaman" (the "a" and "c" standing for Mike's second and third names) was to let the censor know which "Mike" was the writer.

¤

London.

September 30th
Went up to London and we slept in an air-raid shelter at headquarters. Mary is in just the same position as me over India. She polished her sand-brown all day.[178]

¤

October 3rd

Sarsina, Italy.

At this time, fighting as a captain with the Lovat Scouts in the Italian Campaign, was a very special 25-year-old of whom I was to know nothing until the War was over: Alastair "Sandy" Hugh Fraser of Moniack Castle, Kirkhill.

In early 1946 the Lovat Scouts were to move to Greece in support of the Greek Government against the communist insurgency led by the Democratic Army of Greece. Sandy would become Acting Colonel in Greece, and resign his commission in 1967 with the rank of Major. We were not to

---

[178] This was Mary Grant. "Sand-brown" is the nickname for the Sam Browne girdle invented in the 1860s by British Indian Army officer of horse General Sir Samuel James Browne. The Sam Browne is a wide leather belt supported by a strap passing diagonally over the right shoulder.

Sandy Fraser (second row back, fourth from the left)
among his fellow Lovat Scouts in Italy.
Sandy is shown in the centre of the detail, below.

meet until the late 1940s, but then soon enough Sandy and I would fall in love and on 1 July 1950 be married in Gloucester. Sandy was awarded the MC in recognition of his "exemplary gallantry during active operations against the enemy" on October 3rd, 1944. The April 28th, 1945, Highland News *reported Sandy's award and citation thus:*

On October 3rd, 1944, Captain Fraser led a patrol which encountered enemy on Mount Tietra in the Sarsina area. He and two of his party were the first to meet the enemy. Without hesitation he went straight for the wood where they were hiding and drove them out into the open where they were shot down by light machine-gun fire. He then personally led a party to attack the house where the remainder of the enemy were located. Here a grenade was thrown at him, narrowly missing him and he was again fired at from close range, but with complete disregard for his own safety he carried on and succeeded in driving about 10 enemy out of the house, the majority of whom were also killed in the open by light machine-gun fire. The enemy then brought down mortar fire, but Captain Fraser remained with two of his patrol who had been wounded and helped to carry them back safely to our lines. His patrol succeeded in killing or seriously wounding at least 11 enemy, while our own casualties were two wounded, both of whom were brought home.

¤

Dall House on Loch Rannoch, Perthshire.

Philippa's Dad, Sir Anselm Guise, at Dall House with a "royal" – meaning the stag was a twelve-pointer – which he shot. The stag's head is now hanging in Elmore Court.

October 15th

Churchill is in Moscow, everyone hopes for dramatic changes, Aachen is being razed to the ground by the Americans. The Canadians are battling round Arnhem and Antwerp. In Italy the Gothic Line is proving tough to defend. We have landed in Greece and freed the south of the country. Hungary is suing for peace. The Russians are advancing through Rumania. They have also taken Riga. In the Far East we have been bombing Formosa.

October 16th

I am at Dall and went stalking with Dad today. I love being at Dall.

Househill, Nairn.

October 18th

Finally back again at Househill and I wonder what my future is going to be.

November 7th

Sandy Balgonie is here on embarkation leave, Geordie is already in Holland. In the evening we played racing demon. I am studying mechanics in Inverness.

November 10th

Roosevelt has been elected again for the fourth time. Marvellous. Churchill, Roosevelt and Stalin are known as the Big

Three. Churchill in Paris at the moment. The French giving him a great welcome. Very little heard of Hitler. No speech for the usual beer celebrations. Some wonder whether he is dead.

November 13th

The Tirpitz has been sunk. The Last German battleship.

December 1st

In Holland the troops are still bogged down by rain and snow. The Russians are making progress through Hungary and Yugoslavia. Every time we have liberated a country there is a revolution. Greece, Belgium, France, Italy and even Spain and of course Poland too. In most cases the resistance refuse to surrender. There is a lot of talk about democratic communism etc etc.

December 31st

Summary of War. The invasion of course has overshadowed the whole year. First of all the speculation as to when it would take place. Then the shock and jubilation of the actual fact. Then talk of victory in a few weeks. And now the dull depressing slogging. Churchill as popular as ever. Fighting our way up Italy. Dreadful struggle at Cassino, finally captured Rome, June 4, and swept ahead.

Then June 6 D-Day with in the first week both Churchill and the King on the beaches of Normandy. The Falaise Pocket, the hinge of the whole battle. Victory and the great Allies sweep over France, Americans take Paris and we keep the coast, finally entering Brussels. Then slogging on through the floods of Holland. The great airborne disaster of Arnhem, the invasion of southern France, Toulon, and finally the Allied armies facing the whole length of the Siegfried Line. The first German town captured by Americans, Aachen or Aix La Chappelle. An attempt on Hitler's life, confusion in the Reich, all high German generals involved. Hopes running high!

Flying bomb attacks on London, the tragedy of the Guards Chapel. Followed by V2 travelling faster than sound. The Russians first took Leningrad and then swept ahead across the border of Poland, finally halting just before Warsaw, the unfortunate rising of the Poles in the capital before their heroic stand. The Russians enter east Prussia, Romania and Bulgaria sue for peace. And finally now there is a terrific battle for Budapest still in progress. Strikes in industry in this country perfectly intolerable. Churchill goes to Moscow, hopes run high.

We land successfully in Greece. Then the troubles begin, Greek fights Greek. We try to keep order. The ELAS trying to snatch

1944 the power, which develops into a battle for Athens, General Scobie in command. Churchill and Eden go to Athens. Much criticism. However we are now at last in control of Athens and resolved upon a democratic government chosen by the people of Greece.

Nearly every occupied country of Europe that has now been freed is in a great state of disorder. De Gaulle in control of France, Belgium none too quiet. As for poor Poland we now recognise the Government, in London and in Russia. In these countries there seem to be numerous factions. Our enormous and crushing air attacks have remorselessly continued throughout the whole year on Germany and in close support of the Allied armies.

Roosevelt was re-elected for the fourth time, great jubilation. He, Churchill and Stalin known as the Big Three. Churchill in Paris, crowds roar welcome to him. Eisenhower Supreme Allied Commander, Montgomery and Alexander both made Field marshals. All very popular.

The last month of the year dreadful. Bad weather, all the armies bogged down. And the Air Force grounded. Suddenly German offensive in the Ardennes. Regained much ground. German recovery. We have at last stopped the advance but fighting all round the salient.

The Pacific War has gone well with the Americans landing on Leyte and Luzon. And we have steadily fought our way through Burma. On the whole I suppose a successful year. But hopes ran too high, peace before Christmas . . !

1945

January 1st
The toast is Victory this New Year. Everyone is very bored with the War.

January 11th
I am going to join the Red Cross and drive an ambulance.

London.

January 22nd
I am now in the Red Cross and driving an ambulance during the doodlebug raids in London. I am to be posted to Chester.

Chester, Cheshire.

January 24th
I am enjoying the Red Cross. The girls are vey nice. I liked in particular Pooh Allsop. I am duty driver.

January 25th

Took German POWs to Knutsford. These Germans look a pretty tough lot. The Russians now eight miles from Berlin. We have at last reduced the German bulge and now face the whole length of the Siegfried Line and of course still Italy.

¤

Chester.

I was a great friend of my former headmistress' nephew, Alan Ross, who joined the Royal Navy. Who knows where friendship ends and love begins, especially in time of war? When he was in the Navy, Alan wrote me many friendly letters but here is one that was rather different for both of us.

Philippa in Chester, in Red Cross uniform with Alan Ross.

Dear Philippa

Last night I think I said I was in love with you. I could not expect you to give me an answer to that straight away.

Neither of us are sure what that means.

So I would rather say I love you and you love me. And I love you more. That is how it should be and I like it.

love from

Alan

¤

February 1st

I have been put on the Liverpool repats job.[179] Drove there through the Mersey Tunnel, a convoy of 20. We went on to the docks and saw them coming ashore. Some have been prisoners for more than four years, of course all are medically unfit. We had four stretcher cases in our ambulance. Pooh drove and I sat in the back. They all had most tragic tales to tell. They could talk of nothing else, but the horror of their experience. One man had his leg amputated without an anaesthetic. His comrade was shot. One man's wife had been killed by a bomb in London.

---

[179] British repatriated prisoners of war, all wounded, were met at Liverpool Docks by ambulances.

February 5th

We had another trip to Liverpool Docks meeting repats. A band played all sorts of tunes and we all cheered and sang. The Canadians were really funny. They did the Congo and the High Kick up and down the docks to the amusement of the men. We arrived at 5.30 and did not get four stretcher cases till 11.30.

February 6th

At last I have been given an ambulance of my own. I am duty driver. Took some officers to Chester. It is awful knowing people have lost their husbands and fiancés. War is a dreadful thing.

February 12th

Pooh and I went into Chester and saw *Our Hearts Were Young and Gay*. Were nearly sick with laughing so much. Churchill, Stalin and Roosevelt have met at the Black Sea, to end the war and settle some of the peace agreements.

February 13th

We are on an American job. Marvellous organization and efficiency. Met the hospital train and took them to Saighton. Pretty badly wounded lot. Not in bed till 2am.

February 20th

I am now stationed in Prestatyn. Made a friend of Paddy, who is 28.

March 2nd

I took the ambulance to collect Major Manning, staff and Precious. We all had a drink and a merry chat. Major Manning very Irish, like Paddy. Precious very nice and kind. He kissed me. I like him.

The staff of Philippa's ambulance in Prestatyn. Philippa sits on the bonnet (right) with Paddy (left). Centre front, pointing at the dog, is Philippa's boyfriend, Walter Precious.

March 8th

I see Precious every evening now. We went to the flicks in Rhyl.

Philippa with her first boyfriend, Walter Precious, a corporal in the Royal Engineers.

March 9th

The war cannot last much longer now. Cologne has fallen to us. Both the Americans and Canadians are advancing over the Rhine.

March 15th

Went to see Ingrid Bergman in *For Whom the Bell Tolls*. I am told I look like her and I feel very flattered.

March 17th

Didn't have a trip till midnight, when I had drunk quite a lot, because it is St Patrick's Day and Major Manning was there. I had a good conversation with Precious.

March 30th

The Russians going in on the East. They are now advancing on Vienna. Monty has crossed the Rhine and is now 70 miles the other side, not much left of Germany.

April 12th

The news is good, victory a certainty. The Russians have taken Vienna and Königsberg. The Italian line on the move again. Americans 55 miles from Berlin. Still hard work in Holland. We are advancing on Bremen and Leipzig.

April 13th

President Roosevelt died suddenly last night. A very great shock to the world. Granny Guise's funeral at Elmore today. Very sad. We all hope to go to the memorial service in Gloucester Cathedral.

May 1st

After many rumours the marvellous news came that Germany at 6am this morning signed the unconditional surrender. My God, it is unbelievable. Europe at peace, peace. No more bloodshed. Precious and I stood in each other's arms and kissed.

May 8th

V.E. Day. Victory in Europe. Is it possible? Churchill spoke at 6 o'clock. Short and stirring. Ending with "Long Live Britannia" and then "God Save the King". Then we heard all the cheering crowds in London. Fireworks all the evening here.

June 4th

Dick has been posted to Burma. Mary very upset.[180] It brought home to me how difficult I shall find parting with Precious. We went to Holywell today and saw *Kismet* and wandered around everywhere.

June 9th

Dante won the Derby today and Major Manning won £120. He took the staff out for the evening and he got very drunk.

---

[180] Philippa's friend Mary Lamont had developed strong feelings for this serviceman who was not the Dick Allhusen mentioned on October 3rd, 1943. Mary (in nurse uniform) and Dick are the couple on the left of the photograph on page 117.

8

The War Diary: aged 19

June 10th

I'm 19. Paddy's man is back home again, they were engaged before the war, she says he is still marvellous and they will get married. Wonderful. Precious took me out to supper in the Mostyn Hotel and we then went to *Hotel Berlin*. Tomorrow, Sunday, we are going to Llandudno.

June 18th

I am on duty all day, had a case of diphtheria, Paddy had one with meningitis, he was difficult to control.

July 18th

Mum wrote and said Aunt Di has died, she had TB.[181] I am very, very sad. Precious was very sweet to me and took me for a long walk.

July 29th

On duty all day. The welfare officer came, I asked her about being posted abroad and apparently there is quite a possibility. This

[181] Di had died two days before this entry, in Cirencester, aged 54. She was to be buried at Elmore. In 1948 her widower Ardern married a fellow Justice of the Peace, Susan Meath Baker (birth name Madeleine Bryan).

place closes in September. It is also possible I could get back into the FANYs. Of course, spent the evening with Precious.

July 30th

Precious and I went to see *Meet Me in St Louis*. Walked back the long way and then sat and talked for a long time.

August 2nd

Went to see Bob Hope in *The Princess and the Pirate*. Precious says he loves me more than anything.

August 7th

The Atomic bomb was dropped on Japan yesterday. Horrific new invention. Terrifying. The greatest possible weapon of destruction. Probably will revolutionize the world.

August 15th

Today is VJ day. The Japs have agreed to surrender unconditionally. It is extraordinary to think the war is over far sooner than we had expected. Of course the Atom bomb did the trick.

August 25th

What a day. Telephone call, we are to report plus ambulance and kit back to HQ. When I first heard it I felt really sick and then burst into tears and told Precious.

August 26th
I simply can't believe I am to leave Prestatyn and leaving Precious. It seems impossible.

Chester, Cheshire.

August 29th
I hate HQ, a mass of giggling girls. However Precious came over to see me.

August 30th
I was orderly today, in the evening I went to Precious in Rhyl.

September 1st
Did maintenance in the pit under my ambulance. Precious came over to see me in Chester. We walked up the river, beautiful, we came back in a barge down the canal to Llandudno, it was large and horse-drawn.

September 8th
I was on duty all day and couldn't see Precious.

London.

September 13th
The alarm went off at 4.30, our ambulance convoy drove down to London. It was pitch dark, the roads deserted, we drove through little old villages.

Prestatyn, Flintshire.

September 15th

Returned to dear old Prestatyn. Precious met me, stayed up with him till 4am and finally got to bed, really tired.

September 17th

We went to see *My Pal Wolf* and then I had to return to Chester.

Chester, Cheshire.

September 18th

We went to *Blithe Spirit.*

Shrewsbury, Shropshire.

September 20th

A convoy of 10 of us went to Shrewsbury and ferried Italians about. Went shopping.

Flintshire and Caernarfonshire.

September 22nd

Took 9am train, Precious met me in Rhyl and we went to Betws-y-Coed, where we stayed the night. Had glorious walks over to the Conway Falls, but horribly sad because we are rapidly reaching the day of farewell. I know I can't stay with him, it would upset Mum and Dad too much.

October 3rd

Final day has come. I am demobbed. Caught the train via Crewe to Blair Athol, Dad is stalking at Dall. Capt. Wentworth is wonderful. He is now 82.

October 4th

I went with Dad stalking all day in the Corrie and Glen Lyon. Kennedy, the stalker, is a fine astute hill-man. The mist came down and there we were the wrong side of the wind. So no beast today.

October 7th

Did really quite a successful sketch in the Black Wood.[182] I love being at Dall.

October 23rd

I think the news is now almost more depressing than the bad times during the war. These selfish dockers are all still out on strike, while the country starves. Russia disagrees with everything Britain and America say. The British and Americans have led talks and seem to have arrived at deadlock, most countries are having a revolution not to speak of the Jewish-Arabian problems.

---

[182] The Black Wood of Rannoch.

Cumberland.

October 30th

Took train to Penrith. I could hardly control my excitement at last got to Keswick and there was Precious standing on the platform. Oh! How wonderful life is. We are staying at the Royal Oak in two very nice little rooms. We synchronized immediately. Lots to talk about and lots of laughing. Oh so sadly said goodbye.

9

After the War: Art and Love

1946 to 1950

After the War Aunt Bunny inherited Househill and I went to live in London with my parents at 32 Eaton Place, which my mother inherited. I was a sort of Deb and first of all studied art at the Chelsea Polytechnic, and then painting portraits in oils taught by Sonia Mervyn in her studio.

After a few years Geordie Leslie-Melville became my boyfriend and I was once again happy. [183]

[183] See footnote to April 29th, 1941.

Philippa's boyfriend Geordie Leslie-Melville fishing on the Findhorn.

I was happier still when I met Sandy Fraser, to whom I became engaged, and whom I married on July 1st, 1950.

Among those invited to the wedding in Gloucester was Fräulein Weiss, my beloved governess who had gone home to

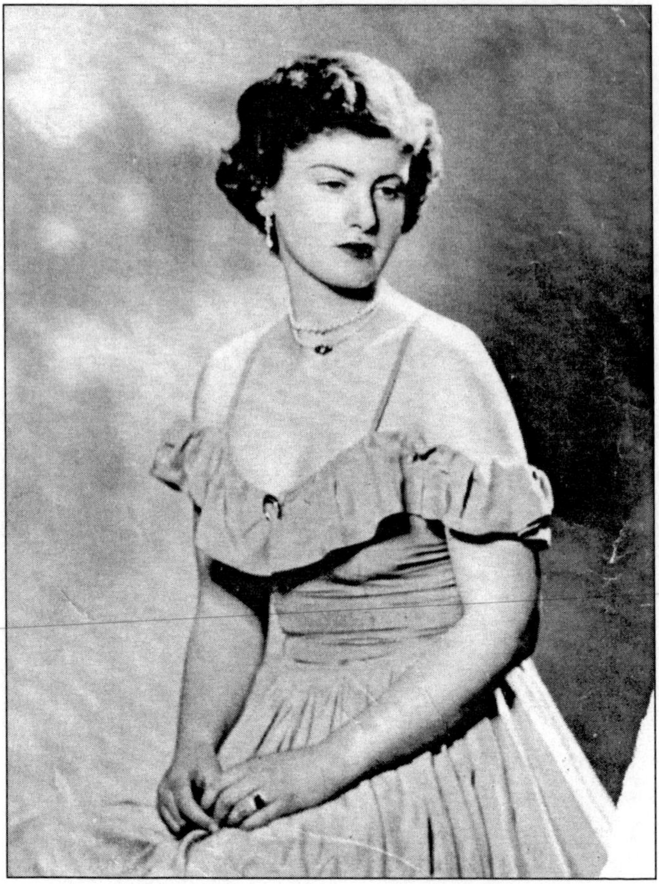

Philippa's 1950 engagement photograph,
taken by society photographic studio Lenare.

Germany in 1939 and been unable to return. On June 5th, 1950, Fräulein Weiss wrote to me with her apologies. Here follows her letter:

¤

5 Juni 1950 *Göttingen*
Merkelstrasse 2

My dearest Philippa, when I got yesterday the announcement of your coming marriage on July 1st I was very happy. Of course, there was, silly enough, one drop of sadness mixed between that. My dear, Philippa, as I have you still in my mind, is now going away from the well known surroundings in which I visited her in my mind; is now stepping out, and establishes her own home. May he make you very very happy. Where shall you live? Where will you spend your honeymoon? He is called Alastair. Does that not mean Scotch? I was thinking that you would be married in Elmore church where your father is patron. Or have you become Roman Catholic?

I should love to see you as a bride and the two boys now grown up men but, alas, I won't be able to come over to England, though several of my friends would put me up. I always hoped that John, having been stationed at Lübeck could come and see me. Tell your fiancé that he has chosen a very nice dear girl.

Heaps of love from your
very loving C. Weiss.

¤

BARONETS DAUGHTER

Mr. Alistair Hugh Fraser, son of the late Major, the Hon. A. J. Fraser, of Lovat and Lady Sybil Fraser, and his bride, Miss Philippa Margaret Guise, daughter of Sir Anselm and Lady Guise, of Elmore Court, Hardwicke, leave St. Peter's Church, Gloucester, after their wedding.

Sandy and Philippa Fraser's wedding
reported in the Gloucester press.

10

Back to the Beginning

September 3rd, 1939

Britain declared war against Germany on September 3rd, 1939. On that same day a 22-year-old Hugh Stirling had written to his first cousin (my future husband), Sandy Fraser, at Sandy's home of Moniack Castle, Kirkhill. Sandy was two-and-a-half years younger than Hugh. Both young men were grandsons of Simon Fraser, 13th Baron Lovat – the Lord Lovat, clan Chief of the Highland Frasers – and had been schoolboys together at Ampleforth College and students at Oxford University.

Here follows Hugh's letter to Sandy, sent on the day that changed their world for ever.

¤

COTTERSTOCK HOUSE,
HELSBY,
CHESHIRE
Sept. 3rd

My dear old horse,

I suppose you have been called up; well, just a line before you go gadding off to the trenches – that is to say, if you haven't already gone. Don't you think this war is an absolutely hellish business? Pardon the moderation of my language, but I never know who may get hold of any letter I write to you.

I really don't know what I'm going to do yet; having been a great slacker and not joined the Territorials, I suppose I need do nothing for the moment, till this conscription bill comes in, but my conscience pricks me towards enlisting in some service or other, and that I shall probably do.

Gone are the halcyon days of Oxford, Sandy old man, and I fear, gone for ever. Which reminds me – what are we going to do about our wireless? I was thinking of selling the thing back to Russell and Phereby, making a spot of money for us both; you observe how the lure of money possesses me even in these difficult days. Or if you want it at Moniack, I'll sell out my share of it to you! There's a good bargain for you! But let me know about it and I'm quite seriously thinking of selling it.

I have only just returned from the Lake District, where I had the most marvellous time, with no news of wars atrocities at all, apart from the essential fact that war hadn't yet broken out. The weather was good this time too. Incidentally your fears that I didn't have a good time at Moniack were quite ungrounded, as I always have a good time there, rain or no rain, even though the weather and your early departure did remove a little of the gilt off the ginger-bread – if that metaphor can be used in such a context.

Well cheerio old horse, all the best; drop me a line as soon as possible, and if we can get a glimpse of each other so much the better.

Yours
Hugh

¤

Hugh's father, Brigadier General Archibald Stirling of Keir, had begun his own military career in the Scots Guards. Hugh followed that same path; and it was as a lieutenant in the 2nd Battalion Scots Guards that, in Libya on April 20th, 1941, he was killed in action. [184]

Hugh has no known grave and so is listed on the Land Forces panels of the Alamein Memorial at the entrance to the Commonwealth War Graves Commission's El Alamein War Cemetery in Egypt.

¤

[184] This date is recorded by the Commonwealth War Graves Commission, though other sources claim he died two days later. Among Hugh's brothers was David Stirling who went on to found the S.A.S.

11

"Best wishes to you for 1940."

January 3rd, 1940

In August, 1940, while 13-year-old Philippa was at Househill, bombs fell on Eastington village, some eight miles south of her Elmore home. Eastington Park was the family home of decorated World War One veteran Claude de Lisle Bush, a family friend known to Philippa as Uncle Claude.

Here follows a New Year letter to Philippa from "Uncle Claude", several months before Eastington was bombed, and only a year before Claude himself was killed in action aged 47.[185]

¤

EASTINGTON PARK,
STONEHOUSE,
GLOUCESTERSHIRE

TELEGRAMS, EASTINGTON.
STATIONS, STONEHOUSE. M.R & G.W.
TELEPHONE, STONEHOUSE 179.

Jan 3rd 1940

Dear Philippa.

Thank you so much for your Christmas card, very dear of you to do it. We are having

[185] For more on "Uncle Claude" see the footnote to August 27th, 1940.

very cold weather here and they are all skating at Frampton.[186] *No hunting and all the small roads covered with ice and snow. It looks like going on and I expect you are having the same. I am sending you a very mixed collection of cigarette cards. Do you still collect them? We have Godfrey back here on six days leave from the Navy.*[187]

Best wishes to you for 1940.

from

Uncle Claude.

---

[186] Eastington is 2½ miles southeast of the village of Frampton-on-Severn, which has three ponds. For more on the severe winter weather, see the entries for January 20th and 24th, 1940.

[187] Claude's son Christopher Godfrey de Lisle Bush had been promoted to rank of Lieutenant on December 1, 1939, and from August 31st, 1942 was to be given command first of HMS Leamington, then HMS Newmarket (both destroyers), lastly the escort destroyer HMS Hambledon. Godfrey would retire from the Navy as a Lieutenant Commander in 1949.

12

Guises and Grants

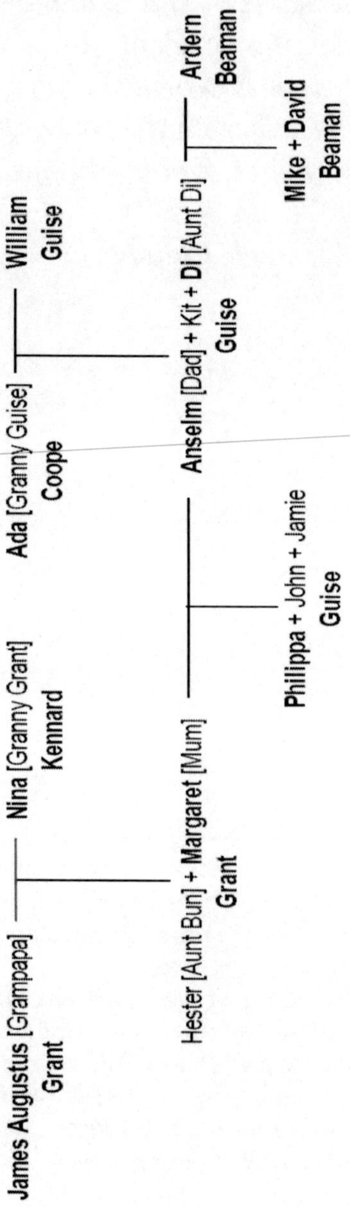

James Augustus [Grampapa] Grant
Nina [Granny Grant] Kennard
Ada [Granny Guise] Coope
William Guise
Hester [Aunt Bun] + Margaret [Mum] Grant
Anselm [Dad] + Kit + Di [Aunt Di] Guise
Ardern Beaman
Philippa + John + Jamie Guise
Mike + David Beaman